**Books from Life Is Amazin**

**Fiction**
Portsmouth Fairy Tales for Gro
Day of the Dead (anthology)
By Celia's Arbour, A Tale of Portsmouth Town
(by Walter Besant and James Rice)
Dark City (anthology)
The Snow Witch, A Portsmouth Novel


**Non-Fiction**
Ten Years In A Portsmouth Slum
(by Robert Dolling)
The History of Portsmouth
(by Lake Allen)
Recollections of John Pounds
(by Henry Hawkes)
Portsmouth, A Literary And Pictorial Tour
(by Matt


**Humour / Novelty**
A Pompey Person's Guide to Everything Great About
Southampton
Southampton Person's Guide to Everything Great About
Portsmouth

# POMPEY WRITES:
# THE BEST OF STAR & CRESCENT (SO FAR)

## EDITED BY
## TOM SYKES AND SARAH CHEVERTON

*Life Is Amazing*

A Life Is Amazing Paperback

Pompey Writes

First published 2018 by Life Is Amazing
www.lifeisamazing.co.uk
ISBN: 978-0-9956394-7-8
First Edition

A catalogue record for this book is available from the British Library

Cover Design: Dan McCabe
Typesetting: Matt Wingett
Cover Image: Dan McCabe

*For Gareth Rees (1948-2018), a troubadour of the vastness, a great friend to Star & Crescent and a wise, decent, wonderful man.*

# Contents

# Introduction

## Sarah Cheverton and Tom Sykes

*The Star and Crescent website was born of frustration with the local media, which too often duplicates the official line of people in power and neglects the views and values of citizens.*

In 2015, the Media Reform Coalition reported that just six companies own over 80% of local newspapers – and the Johnstone Press, which runs *The News* here in Portsmouth, has swallowed up most of these titles. Corporate ownership is subject to a conflict of interests between the need for journalists to hold power to account and the imperative to deliver ever larger profits to shareholders. The decision by *The News* to run two front-page wraparound advertisements in support of the Conservative Party ahead of the 2017 General Election is an egregious example of this dilemma.

In addition to commercialisation, the impact of digital publishing on the local print media is a further challenge. The researcher Rasmus Kleis Nielson wrote in 2015, 'The business models that local newspapers have been based on are under tremendous pressure today as readership is eroding, advertising declining, and overall revenues plummeting. Digital growth has far from made up for what has been lost on the print side of the business. Most newspaper companies have responded by cutting costs to remain profitable or at least limit the operating losses.'

These cuts have had a devastating effect on local and regional news. According to the Press Gazette, there has been a net loss of almost 200 newspapers in the UK since 2005 and during this period the number of journalists has halved. The National Union of Journalists (NUJ) reported in March 2017 that over 400 local journalism jobs had been lost in the preceding 17 months alone.

The NUJ have charted the impact of these cuts in their campaign Local News Matters:
'These cuts pose a threat to local democracy:
- local politicians are not being held to account,
- voters are not being given a range of views and
- voters are deprived of the information they require to make judgements when voting in elections.'

We need local newspapers to ensure accountability and to encourage informed and active citizenship.

This is where *Star & Crescent* came in. When we started in February 2015, we were a small collective of writers and editors frustrated by the lack of scrutiny towards Portsmouth policy-makers and political representatives, as well as by the declining quality of local news.

Our aims from the beginning were (and they remain the same today) to:

- Hold power to account
- Provide a platform on which to raise up missing and marginalised voices
- Inspire debate about the real issues that affect local people
- Increase local interest and involvement in politics
- Promote the city as a lively, creative and cultural place to live, work and study

In the last three years, we have done this in a number of ways:

- Publishing voices that are not otherwise heard in the mainstream media – from residents in our poorest communities to local activists
- Using satire to bring politics to a wider audience
- Acting as a platform for local investigative reporting
- Sharing voices from across the political spectrum
- Regularly publishing local poets and authors
- Sharing the untold and little-known aspects of Portsmouth's history

We've worked with hundreds of residents, local writers, organisations and activists to bring you stories that the mainstream media is not generally interested in. We've covered a wide range of issues including mental health, homelessness, housing, domestic violence and austerity. We've built a network of Portsmouth satirists and we've published reviews of Portsmouth's ever-expanding cultural scene. Our regular Poems, Portsmouth Writers' Season and Pompey Stories sections have provided a platform for talented creative writers.

As a small team of volunteers with no core funding but with some donor support, we've achieved a lot in the last three years. We got our first scoop in 2016 – the still shameful tale of Conservative councillor Scott Harris' plan to smear three local residents active in opposing Tory cuts – which was later picked up by the national press. We've supported our community by taking part in the campaign against cuts to Portsmouth City Council's domestic violence services and publicising the work of community activists like Kimberly Barrett in raising awareness about how property developers are avoiding their responsibility to provide Portsmouth people with affordable housing.

But we've also had victories beyond Portsmouth. We were included in the Bureau of Investigative Journalism's Twitter round-up of community news in 2017 for our coverage of fire safety in Portsmouth's high-rise buildings following the Grenfell Tower fire. As Editor-in-Chief, Sarah Cheverton has travelled to India, Sweden and Norway to talk to journalists from across the world about *S&C* and the possibilities offered by independent media to challenge the growing crisis in the mainstream news, as part of the Digital Identities programme funded by Google News Labs. In 2016, our Features Editor and co-founder Tom Sykes, addressed a group of media students at De La Salle University in the Philippines about *S&C*'s relevance to young people and the issues they care about. We have also become part of a growing number of hyperlocals signing up to independent press regulator Impress and were early members of the Independent Community News Network created by the Centre for Community Journalism in Cardiff.

So, it is with great pride that we have now recorded S&C's greatest moments – plus some new, never previously published material – in the book you are now holding. Read on for insightful reporting and commentary on local culture, media, ecology, housing, healthcare, education and gender issues plus first-rate poetry, short fiction, travel writing, satire and visual art.

We've worked hard to make this anthology as extensive and essential as possible. We hope you will read, enjoy, think about the issues raised and ask tough questions of those in positions of power and influence!

POMPEY WRITES

### *Star & Crescent* Anthem
### Will Sutton (2018)

Spice Island
Whale Island
Highland Road Cemetery
Sallyport
Legography
Aspex Gallery
Flat White in Southsea
Ferryboat from Gosport'll
lead you to New Theatre Royal
or St James Hospital


No. 6, Love Bugs,
Model village, steam tugs
Mozzarella Joe's
Spillage of Mary Rose
Canoe Lake
Tenth Hole cake
Toilets closed on Albert Road
Conan Doyle in Fratton Goal
Harbour crash, Ark Royal


*A politician's jag*
*While Eastney sewers clag*
*Delivering your daily dag*
          *It's Star & Crescent rag*

Geological erosion
Museum of Explosion
Charles Dickens' Birthplace
Astrium, Art Space
Kipling, Gaiman, HG Wells
Langstone harbour tide smells
Portsdown Hill, Still & West
Tricorn Centre stairs left
Pie & Vinyl, Wedgewood gigs
Hilsea Lido, Pyramids
Sundays at the Bandstand
Yarn-bombing, Akram's
Tall ships, splash park
Graffiti by MyDog & Farkfk
Hovercraft, mainsail
Portchester Castle
Strolls along the sea 'n'
D-Day Museum
Pompey Pluckers
Beach hut brollies
Spitbank Fort
Palmerston's Follies
M275
Action Stations
sailors' wives
tattoos on the Hard and
Southsea Rose Garden

*Was it councillors on the blag*
*Or Isis selling skag*
*crashed our website defrag*
        *@SandCPompey# ?*

Naked people Eastney Beach
Million Pebbles numbered each
King's Theatre, mudlarks
Seaside kisses after dark
Square Tower, Round Tower
Submarines with nuclear power
Foghorn calls, Hotwalls,
Spinnaker Tower

QA, TeaTray
Eastney Cellars, RMA
Clarence Pier, Kite Fair,
Guildhall graduation day
Gunwharf bars, Aquacars
Peter Sellers, Mountbatten
Please move down, front 4 cars
The platform's short at Fratton

*Was it diplomatic brags?*
*MPs who don't give a shag?*
*Look up to Portsdown's crag*
*for the Star & Crescent flag*

## Portsmouth's Smeargate: Dirty Politics in the Age of Austerity

### Sarah Cheverton and Tom Sykes (2016)

*Star & Crescent* was the first media outlet to report on a leaked email sent by Conservative councillor Scott Harris in which he expressed that 'it might be a good idea to play dirty' in the 2016 local elections.

In the email – sent to all Portsmouth's Conservative councillors – Harris revealed that he was 'compiling some stuff' on Jon Woods, a social worker for Portsmouth City Council (PCC) and a trade union activist; on Sameen Farouk, a local resident and campaigner; and on Shonagh Dillon, CEO of a local charity, Aurora New Dawn. All three have been active critics of PCC's cuts programme. One of the tactics proposed in the email was a vindictive complaint to Farouk's employer, with the intention of getting him dismissed from his job.

After the story broke, Harris faced calls to resign and apologised for his conduct (but only to Farouk). Despite this, local Conservative councillors have continued to make negative statements about Farouk and Aurora New Dawn.

Council leader Donna Jones described Farouk's behaviour as 'horrific' in an interview with the Portsmouth *News*. The reason why? Mr Farouk had submitted Freedom of Information requests on a variety of local issues, none of which have been deemed 'vexatious' by the council (the mechanism by which local authorities can challenge FOI requests that are frequent, offensive, or overly burdensome). Readers unfamiliar with the regulations and processes around FOIs were implicitly encouraged to believe the leader was right to assess as 'horrific' a citizen's democratic right to interrogate the decisions of local government.

Jones also made a series of false claims in *The News* about Aurora New Dawn, a Hampshire charity working with victims of domestic and sexual violence. She said that the charity was complicit in a 'hate campaign' when in fact it was simply questioning the wisdom of reducing the council's specialist service for domestic violence victims by £180,000 without any clear plans to safeguard victims and their families.

Despite the campaign against cuts to domestic violence services clearly involving a range of partners – it is led by national direct action group Sisters Uncut and supported by the End Violence Against Women coalition, trade unions and *Star & Crescent* – Conservative councillor Rob New, the cabinet member responsible for cuts to domestic violence services, has also targeted Aurora New Dawn.

He singled out Shonagh Dillon for 'orchestrating a campaign of protest' and implied she was involved in direct action taken by Sisters Uncut at a council meeting in December 2015. According to New, Dillon used 'her domestic abuse provider [sic] to further a hurricane of disruption that was led by Sisters Uncut against this city council.'

Like Jones, New offered no evidence for his claims and was quickly proven wrong when a Sisters Uncut spokesperson stated that they were solely responsible for the direct action.

Whilst the accusations made by Portsmouth councillors are no doubt damaging on their own terms, together they reveal the presence of a more worrying trend, with serious implications for local democracy.

Jones attacked the protest against council cuts by stating that 'we have had democracy compromised in Portsmouth.' She was joined in this sentiment by John Ferrett, the right-wing leader of Portsmouth's Labour group, who have entered into an informal coalition with the Conservatives and UKIP in Portsmouth and chosen to abstain on the most recent cuts. 'I'm not a fan of direct action in a democracy,' Ferrett tweeted.

This demonstrates a breath-taking ignorance of local politics. Almost all political progress made in the history of Portsmouth – from pamphleteering against the corruption of the monarchy in the 1810s to university students disrupting arms industry events two centuries later – has been won by 'ordinary' people standing up to elite interests, often by taking direct action.

A more critical observer might conclude that rather than local residents and a charity disrupting local democracy, it is being compromised by Portsmouth councillors themselves. When public servants like Scott Harris refuse to resign despite being caught conspiring against the very people they are supposed to represent, then local politicians start to look as arrogant, self-serving and disconnected as their national counterparts when they accept cash for questions or waste public money on cleaning their moats.

Thanks to the eccentricities of our electoral system, the Tories narrowly won the 2015 General Election with only 24% of the eligible vote. Jones and other Tories conclude from this that their austerity agenda has broad public support. So, when they make damaging cuts that directly contradict the will and needs of local people, nobody should be surprised when groups like Sisters Uncut resort to peaceful direct action as the only available democratic platform left. That local councillors are quick to attack political resistance by the electorate to their policies as abuse, as 'horrific' and as somehow against the ethos of democracy itself speaks to a level of privilege and power that should concern us all.

Yet perhaps these actions are less surprising in a political landscape where the Prime Minister responds to criticism over closing children's centres by telling his opponent to 'put on a proper suit, do up your tie and sing the national anthem.' The electorate are becoming increasingly accustomed to a politics that harnesses insults, insinuation and intimidation instead of evidence-based debate—but at what price?

Whether by chance or design, the worst consequence of the smear campaign in Portsmouth has been to deflect attention away from the real scandal: needless Tory cuts that will almost certainly result in the deaths of more Portsmouth women. Alongside these victims are the voters of Portsmouth who are caught in an elaborate web of 'he said, she said' facilitated and encouraged by the mainstream local press. Far more of a threat to democracy than direct action, this dirty politics is causing the electorate to become ever more disengaged and disenfranchised at a time when it has never been more important to take a stand.

## The Ditty Boy

Denise Bennett (2016)

*Imaginary words written by a sailor on board HMS M33 – Gallipoli 1915*

I lift the lid and find
his whole life harboured here;
things that he kept safe:
    a photo of his wife Mary –
baby daughter Jess – tress
of her hair tied with red ribbon,
    three letters from home
telling news of harvest,
of felling trees in the orchard,
    a picture postcard from Alf
his brother, sent from Plymouth;
Derry's clock decked out in bloom...
    and here's his baccy pouch,
his diary full of pencil sketches
of the ship's cat sleeping,
    and the white starched hankie,
initials embroidered by his sister Doris –
his boot brush and blacking.
    I can see him now, his big hands
buffing and skimming
until he could see his face
    shine in the leather – his happy face.
I pack up his pen and pipe,
his wash things...
    stow his world away
to send to his widow and Jess –
and all who come after.

## Star and Crescent, Then and Now

### Richard Brooks (2015)

The star and crescent are ancient symbols of Portsmouth's civic identity. They decorated the seal on the charter that brought the city into legal existence on the 2nd May 1194. But that was over 800 years ago; surely we have come a long way since then? In material terms, perhaps. In other ways, people's concerns remain similar. Many things we now take for granted evolved during the early Middle Ages, which was a less affluent time but not necessarily less moral or cultured. The simple beauty of the twelfth century arches in St Thomas's Cathedral suggest the period when they were built was by no means as primitive or miserable as popular cliché might suggest.

The most striking feature of medieval Portsmouth, or *Portesmue* as it was known, is the lack of people. Today's conglomeration is among the most densely populated in Europe. In the 1080s, William the Conqueror's nationwide survey of who owned what, the *Domesday Book*, counted just over thirty adult males on Portsea Island, perhaps 150 people all told.

Political stability and favourable weather may have trebled those figures by the 1190s. Portsea's habitable area was smaller then. Salt marshes and tidal creeks pushed deep inland, their presence recalled by place names such as Great Salterns or Lake Road. People clustered around St Mary's Parish Church or St Thomas's, just north of the Camber. Both churches were endowed in the late 1100s and stand today as evidence of an emerging sense of community.

Everyday life was frugal then, even for the elite. Fruit was a seasonal delicacy, reserved for high status celebrations. Corn and bacon captured in an early English naval victory at Damme, in modern Belgium, were compared favourably with King Arthur's mythical spoils. In the absence of tea and oranges, people drank weak beer, without hops. Wine was for aristocrats, like the two tuns that Portsmouth's city elders provided for royal use in 1222.

Violence was endemic. Delayed in Portsmouth by adverse winds, Richard I's Welsh and Flemish mercenaries fought each other, forcing the king to interrupt his hunting in Bere Forest to quell the riot. An age devoid of penal institutions, where every man (and some women) went armed, demanded the uncompromising punishments laid down in the early *Customs and Usages of Portsmouth*: dishonest tradesmen faced the pillory; thieves a range of mutilation and homicides death by burning or drowning. If such penalties seem harsh, then consider the corrosive social effects of leaving unpunished the irregularities that contributed to the recent financial crisis.

Occurring within days of the charter, the brawls of May 1194 signalled Portsmouth's emergence as England's premier naval base. Ever since, local fortunes have fluctuated according to the defence budget. W.G. Gates, Portsmouth's pioneering historian, listed fifteen royal visits in the 50 years either side of the charter's issue. Kings of England were also Dukes of Normandy. Like modern ferry operators, they knew the shortest route ran between Portsmouth and Caen, although the passage took longer then. Richard I sailed from Portsmouth in May 1194, never to return; his brother John disembarked there in 1203, after losing his continental inheritance.

Portsmouth prospered at the national expense as John mounted futile expeditions to recover Normandy. In 1205, the Exchequer paid £350 for naval wages and a large mast, a sum representing several years' income for Portsmouth's working population. In 1212, John instructed William Brewer, Sheriff of Hampshire, to erect walls and penthouses around his *esclusa*, now underneath the entrance to Gunwharf Quays, to preserve his ships and related tackle. As usual, peacetime austerity followed wartime plenty. John's fiscally challenged son Henry III paid off his ships, and filled in the dock, to make way for tidal mills.

People's personal needs have left more visible remains. Portsmouth's first hospital was founded in the year King John walled his dockyard. Peter des Roches, Bishop of Winchester, endowed Domus Dei, or God's House, to accommodate pilgrims, and help sick and infirm locals. The layout was functional, similar to other hospitals founded at the same time: a chapel to the east with an adjoining hall, now the chancel and nave of Old Portsmouth's Garrison Church. Patients or guests were disposed either side in the aisles, leaving the centre free, as in a modern hospital ward. Funding was local, from legacies and rents.

Medical treatments were limited, but patients were cared for physically and spiritually, following the Salernitan Rule, a code of nursing practice not always observed today. When William Marshal, who ruled England following John's death, fell ill with bowel cancer little could be done to save him, but he died in the arms of his son and best friend, as assured of salvation as anyone could be. His was an exemplary death, movingly described in his verse biography, a dignified end to which we all might aspire.

On a more mundane level, the thirteenth century was also interested in shopping. A major benefit of King Richard's charter was permission to hold a free market every Thursday. More serious business could be done at the Fair held every August for fifteen days, open to all the king's men from England and Scotland [sic], as well as from Normandy, Anjou, and Poitou. Only recently has Portsmouth once more become part of so wide a free trade area.

Commercial activity depended on local regulation to maintain quality and discourage fraud. By the late 1200s, the borough had a mayor and bailiff, two constables and two clerks, supervised by twelve jurors and a citizens' 'moot'. Formal arrangements ensured a smooth transfer of office every year. At a national level, trade benefited from the first flowering of the rule of law, something not globally assured today. Richard I's father, Henry II, had instituted regular court sessions that evolved into today's county courts. In 1225, Adam of Porteseye was one of the justices appointed to hear cases at Winchester.

These first steps towards freedom within the law sometimes faltered. When things went wrong, the tiny scale of civil society made it hard for the great and not so good to escape popular anger. Left to govern England during Richard's absence on Crusade, William Longchamps, Bishop of Ely, provoked general outrage by his all-encompassing ambition. Gerald of Wales called him 'the many-headed monster'. Fleeing the country dressed as a woman, William was unmasked at Dover by an importunate sailor on the razz, and imprisoned amid much ribaldry. Rehabilitated on Richard's turn, it was Longchamps, as Chancellor of England, who set his seal on Portsmouth's charter with its twin device of star and crescent. Symbols of civic identity, they are also reminders of the transience of political authority, a useful lesson still.

## Pompey:
## No one Comes Near Our Genius

### Reg Chrettyn (2018)

Portsmouth. Isn't it great? Aren't we great? No one comes near us. No one. No mush at all. Especially not the scummers.

What's not to love? Cream tea on the Common. Full English on the Pier. White Lightning on Fratton Road. Salt on your chips. Salt of the earth. Salt in the sea. The Royal Navy. The Royal Marines. Our brave boys on the P&O ferries. Old warships that handed the Frenchies' arses to them in a high hat. A ruddy great tower that looks just like another one in a nasty foreign hell-hole we flog weapons to. Play up Pompey. Cliff the Dancing Man. The Chubb Lock. Bloody brilliant.

Charles Dickens. HG Wells. Rudyard Kipling. Mike Hancock. Colin Galloway. Arnold Schwarzenegger. Donna Jones. Roger Black. Harry Redknapp. (Sort of. For a bit.) Peter Sellers and Peter Griffiths. John Pounds and John Ferrett. Houston Stewart Chamberlain and Richard Chamberlain (possibly). Heroes all. All of them heroes. Them all heroes.

Oh, and Winston Churchill Avenue. The man's a hero, not the road. Obviously.

Problem is, readers, some folk round here aren't heroes. They're the opposite of heroes. They want to wreck our rep. They talk us down. Or they make us look bad. They hate us. They hate themselves. They hate everything. All of it.

Who am I talking about? For starters, the homeless camped outside my gaff. What's that all about, eh? It's outrageous. Having to smell them, I mean. Don't they know they'll drive the house prices down? Get a job. Not that difficult, is it? I'm working class and I managed it.

Blimey.

Then you've got your PC Gestapo telling us what to do. I'll tell them where to go. How about that? SJWs. Social Justice Warriors. Stupid Jobless W*****s, I call 'em. University types. Well, I went to the University of Life and I got a PhD in Pulling Myself Together and Getting the F*** On With It.

That university we got here. Crawling with commies, it is. Like cockroaches, they are. Remember history anyone? The Russian Revolution started with subversive talk of 'knowledge exchange strategies'. Lenin taught business studies. Stalin was a professor of leisure and tourism. Lest we forget. Never forget.

And more to the point, what's the point? Nine grand a year to learn some fancy words with which to bash our Queen and Country. It's a swindle. I tell you.

And where does it get you in the Real World, eh? If I was dictator – which I bloody well should be – I'd bring back conscription. That'd sort them students out. Instead of crawling out of the ivory tower and into the dole queue they'd go and get themselves blown up instead. Young people need that kind of discipline. And if that didn't work I'd bring back hanging. Never did me any harm. Quite enjoyed it. Actually.

Makes you sick doesn't it? And that's the truth.

Never mind climate change. (Another lefty swindle). Never mind Kim Jong what's-his-face. Never mind war, famine, AIDS or Jeremy Corbyn. The biggest threat to our civilisation is political correctness. Gone mad. Utterly bonkers.

I mean, whatever next? Batperson versus Superpansexual? The fur-hatted boys of the PC NKVD raiding my house at dawn and confiscating all my Jim Davidson and Richard B Spencer DVDs? Like to see 'em try, mush.

You know who I'm talking about. It's that lot who've infiltrated all our great local institutions from Her Majesty's Armed Forces to Purbrook Crochet Club. Like rats, they are. That lot with their knock-kneed, limp-wristed hankering not to be beaten to death. For what's basically a lifestyle choice. Sad. Pathetic. Get a life. Not a lifestyle.

Clean your bedroom. Keep your back straight. Are you a man or a mouse? Are you a bird or a bloke? Make your mind up.

You couldn't make it up.

Don't get me wrong. I'm not against it. Don't think people should go to prison for it anymore. But just don't come bothering me with it. Don't follow me into a public toilet, grab me by the shirt-tail, whisper sweet nothings into my earhole and then start singing Village People songs at me. Or you'll get a knuckle sarnie. With a side order of acute pain. With sod-right-off sauce squirted all over it.

It's how Nazi Germany started. I tell you. And Stalinist Russia. And contemporary Southampton. These snowflakes don't understand our way of life. Our freedoms. Our free minds. Our free markets.

If you don't like our austerity, exploitation, Islamophobia, gender pay gaps, neo-imperialist warfare, environmental destruction or our Katie Hopkins then bugger off to Mars with you. That's a red planet, isn't it?

Traitors. Cowards. Ingrates.

It's what we're all thinking but who has the balls to say it?

Donald Trump has the balls. Nice ones, I hear. What a geezer. We need someone like him in our city. Donna Jones is alright but she doesn't go far enough. How far is far enough? Don't know. But Trump would go further.

And that's what we need right now. Otherwise we'll continue to live in some anti-free-speech-liberal-moron's wet dream of 1984. The book, not the year. Obviously.

Sometimes I feel like I'm the only sane one left. Everyone else is on a weekend break to Cloud Cuckoo Land. Except they can't ever come back because the airline's gone into liquidation. And Heathrow Airport's closed down. Because of the bloody unions.

Probably.

I could go on speaking my bonce like this. But is anyone still reading? Did anyone start reading? Maybe all they did was frown at the clickbaity title for a second.

It's okay. I'm used to that.


*Note: 'Reg Chrettyn' is the pen name of Professor Sir Willoughby 'Willy' Montague 'Ginger' Featheringstone-Howe (Baron Featheringstone-Howe of Glumley), a man so upper-class that he has two nicknames. Featheringstone-Howe was educated at Eton College, where he won the Strafford and Bowman Shakespeare Prize, and at All Soul's College, Oxford, where he completed a DPhil in late Victorian Decadent aesthetics. He was elected the youngest fellow of that college since 1527. He currently holds professorial chairs in English Literature at Oxford, Cambridge, Yale and Harvard Universities. He was made a life peer by the British government in 2011.*

## *Dunkirk*: Grand, Bland and Nationalistic

### Stephen Harper (2017)

According to my late mother, my grandad was evacuated on 'the last boat out of Dunkirk'. I didn't discuss this with the old guy before he died – I was too young and lived too far away from him – but after his death I read more about Operation Dynamo and often wondered about his story. Christopher Nolan's much-heralded extravaganza is the latest of several attempts to put that story on the big screen.

It's only fair to begin by saying that I'm no great fan of Nolan's work. I found *Interstellar* (2014) overblown, and several critics have – rightly, I think – identified films such as *The Dark Knight* (2008) and *The Dark Knight Rises* (2012) as politically conservative. Let's just say I prefer Nolan's early work. Nevertheless, stylistically, the new film is innovative and sometimes captivating: throughout *Dunkirk*, sea and sky twist and spiral in a mesmerising kaleidoscope of blue-grey fractals. And Nolan builds tension well, emphasising the soldiers' desperate plight by showing men in various types of trap: Harry Styles and company are trapped in a boat that is being shot at by the enemy; a Spitfire pilot is unable to escape from the cockpit of his sea-ditched plane as the water level rises; a traumatised and unpredictable soldier (Cillian Murphy) is locked inside a room below deck on a rescue boat – and presumably locked inside himself, too. All are encased and in danger.

On the other hand, we are hardly invited to empathise with these imperilled men. The ensemble nature of the film – together with Hans Zimmer's bombastic musical soundtrack – leaves little room for expressions of interiority or, indeed, for any sort of character development; as one might expect from a film shot on 70mm, this is experiential, immersive cinema rather than character-driven drama. Of course, ensemble war films can work well: one thinks here of *The Thin Red Line* (1998), whose metaphysical voiceovers provide a ruminative and arguably subversive perspective on war; but in *Dunkirk* there is no such narrative device to shed light on the soldiers' feelings or thoughts, making this a rather unengaging film at the emotional level.

The film's ideological register, meanwhile, is distinctly British-patriotic. While the opening scene (easily the film's most exciting) fleetingly depicts some glowering Frenchmen manning the town's barricades, the very significant French presence on the beach at Dunkirk is all but ignored (for that side of the story, see Henri Verneuil's superior, irony-laden 1964 film *Weekend at Dunkirk*). Whether in the air with an impossibly deadly Spitfire ace played by Tom Hardy (who single-handedly seems to down the entire Luftwaffe), at sea with saturnine sailor Mark Rylance, or on the beach with the harried and frustrated evacuees, we see through British eyes. At times the national-chauvinist sentiment grates: Rylance, sailing towards a deadly warzone, finds time to wax lyrical about the beauty of the overhead Spitfires 'with their Rolls Royce engines' and the film ends, all too predictably, with the words of Winston Churchill, solemnly read aloud from a newspaper by a returning soldier.

None of the soldiers, meanwhile, expresses a view about the political causes of their plight and there is thus no counterweight to the film's patriotism. Indeed, while *Dunkirk* is a film about an inglorious defeat, the mood slowly lists towards sentimental nationalism (recalling a motif from *Interstellar*, 'Home', as uttered by Kenneth Branagh's naval officer Commander Bolton, becomes the film's most resonant utterance). Evacuated of the French allies, the German enemies, and any political frame of reference beyond Churchillian bluster, Nolan's film feels strangely insular and abstract (perhaps, as the film critic Adam Nayman has suggested, Nolan should be seen as a Platonic rather than a humanist filmmaker). And so, for all its audio-visual *Sturm und Drang*, *Dunkirk* is ultimately a rather tame affair in which character development and political context are sacrificed for grand spectacle and bland sentimentality.

## Hanging Out with the Dream King:
## An Interview with Neil Gaiman

### Sarah Cheverton (2015)

When I meet Neil Gaiman he is sitting on a wooden bench by Canoe Lake in Southsea, the backdrop to one of his earliest and most haunting graphic novels, Mr Punch. He has his back to me and is dressed entirely in black. Chatting to his publicist, I almost don't see him and when I do, my first thought is: 'It's the Sandman.'

Neil turns to us with a broad but tired grin as his publicist tells me to 'make sure he gets a cup of tea.'

It's a warm, sunny day. Neil is on the last leg of an epic signing tour across the USA, Canada and Europe. After 25 years of touring, this is his last. Returning to Portsmouth, where as a boy Neil lived every summer with his grandparents, has an added significance this time. It's the summer and the city has named a road just west of Canoe Lake after his latest book, a decision he says feels 'very unreal in an astoundingly nice way.'

Portsmouth still holds a personal fondness for Neil; he has spent the morning driving around the city, capturing memories. The city's forgotten heritage intertwines with his own in some surprising ways.

His grandfather ran a grocer's store on Charlotte Street, while his Uncle Monty was 'the first bookie in England to take bets on a royal name.' Neil goes on to say, 'The lovely thing about Portsmouth is that it's so gloriously layered, Portsmouth and Southsea. You've got such old, glorious things.'

Gesturing towards Canoe Lake, he says, 'More than anywhere else you could possibly point to in the entirety of the whole, you know, Portchester to Purbrook to Southsea continuum (of Neil's childhood homes), this has the most memories, the happiest memories. Portsmouth for me is fascinating because my first two personal graphic novels, *Violent Cases* and *Mr Punch,* are 100% Portsmouth and Southsea, that's what they are. In many ways, they're a giant sort of brain dump of all of my memories of growing up, including going to peculiar children's parties at one of these seaside hotels.'

By contrast, *The Ocean*, as Neil calls the novel, began as a short story for his wife, rock star Amanda Palmer, which expanded to 'a novelette, a novella, then finally a novel'.

It was a complete departure from Neil's usual writing process, being the first book he's written without knowing the ending from the start – and without planning to write a novel in the first place.

Despite his misgivings, the book debuted at number one in the *New York Times* bestseller list in 2013, surprising its author in becoming one of his most popular books yet.

'The odd thing is that in my head, I didn't expect it to be either the critical or the commercial success it's become,' he says, expecting instead that the book would be 'one of these things I do that are vaguely approved of but don't really change the world.'

Fans and critics have attributed much of the book's success to the authentic characterisation of its narrator, who Neil has admitted is, essentially, his seven-year-old self.

'It was a weird kind of rollercoaster to write, but the weirdest thing about it looking back was spending three months being seven,' he says. 'I was 51 years old and being seven in my head. That was really odd.'

The process was, Neil says, a question of 'running through places' from his childhood 'to the point where I could remember what it smelled like in the weird little outhouse that we stored coal in – mostly damp, and coal. It's stuff that, in many cases, you haven't really thought about since it happened.'

The reception from fans suggests his three months revisiting in the past has paid off.

'I think one of the things I love most about *The Ocean* is the amount of people who've read it and said, "You wrote my childhood and my childhood was nothing like that."'

He smiles and takes a sip of tea, 'It's that weird moment of "Okay, I did something clever here". I think without trying to sometimes, it's almost as if when you can get accurately specific enough, you can somehow become universal.'

One of the biggest dilemmas in writing the novel was deciding on the intended audience. Neil reached a point where 'I had to decide – am I writing a children's book or not?

For me, the key to figuring it out was realising, actually, this book is a lot about helplessness. There's this whole big, adult world and it's big and it's dangerous and inexplicable and unexplained – and you don't get a book of instructions.'

Children, Neil says, 'have to cope as best you can and a lot of the time, you're going to fail.'

The book doesn't flinch from these moments of failure, which is 'particularly, the reason I don't think it's a book for kids. I don't think it's ultimately hopeless. I don't think it's ultimately bleak. The final chapter is incredibly upbeat, but I'm not sure I could show that final chapter to a kid and explain why it's upbeat.'

On the book's back cover, Neil writes that *The Ocean at the End of the Lane* is, he hopes, 'at its heart ... a novel about survival.'

'Talking to people who read the book, it obviously resonates with a lot of them that way,' he says. 'A lot of people have been talking about issues of violence, fear and all the places that childhood gets unsafe.'

This has been a recurring theme in many of his books, from early graphic novels *Violent Cases* and *Mr Punch*, through to children's books such as *Coraline*. He is particularly fascinated by the often thin line between entertaining children and scaring them, from the alarming violence of Punch and Judy to the 'really crap magician who would normally be scary' at children's parties.

As a child, he says, 'I was never able to figure out why would you terrify kids?'

When I ask what scares him, he immediately answers, 'Things happening to my children, something bad happening to my wife.'

And in terms of writing, does someone as successful as Neil Gaiman still get The Fear?

'God, yeah. My editor will tell you about the incredibly apologetic email that I sent her saying, "Look, I've accidentally written a novel. I'm really sorry. You don't have to publish it. It's just a thing I did. Sorry."'

There's only one thing, Neil says, to be done with fear.

'You carry on. When I was a little kid, even into my teens, I thought I was a coward because I got scared. It wasn't until I was in my thirties and thinking about it and I had one peculiar experience that I should probably tell where I realised that I had thought about fear all wrong and I'd thought about bravery all wrong.

'I thought that being brave meant not being scared. There was a sudden moment in my thirties where I trod on an underground wasps' nest and suddenly was surrounded by a crowd of stinging wasps. And I was with my kids, Mike and Holly. Maddie wasn't born yet.

'I just thought, "If I run, the wasps are going to sting the kids, so I shouted at them, urgently, to run and I stayed where I was and I got stung. And when the kids were far enough away, I raced after them."'

'And later on, I got into the bathtub and the kids were there and they counted the stings and there were over 30.

'And what was interesting is I wasn't scared. It didn't even occur to me to be scared. I was just going, "Okay, this is what has to happen right now." But my glasses had fallen off. And so, I realised I had to go back and get them or I would never find them again. So, an hour or so later, I went back to find my glasses and I was terrified.

'And I went back and found my glasses and did not get stung and headed home. And I thought, that was really interesting. It was not brave when I was standing there being stung. People would have said, "It was so brave, he stood there and got stung."

'But no, no bravery involved because it didn't occur to me to be scared. I did what I had to do. The point where I was brave was going back and getting my glasses. That was brave. So, I thought, OK, I've misunderstood this my whole life. Being brave doesn't mean you're not scared. Being brave means you're absolutely, shit-scared, you're terrified but you do the right thing anyway.

'That changed everything for me.'

We drink the last of our tea and prepare to walk back around Canoe Lake to the naming ceremony that will permanently mark the author's impact on our hometown, and on readers across the world.

'It's odd, I'm not scared of dying,' he thinks aloud. 'I don't know if that's because I've been able to write my name on the wall, to feel like I was here. I don't know if people will still be reading me a hundred years from now, or if the things I've done are going to last, but I hope so.'

## The Price of Blackwell's Bookshop and the Value of Nothing

### Matt Wingett (2018)

Sadly, after much imploring, petitioning and dissent among university and townsfolk alike, Blackwell's University Bookshop, Portsmouth has closed down.

The shop has been the most extraordinary hub, with writers launching numerous books there, academics and townsfolk alike mingling and sharing ideas, students supported and helped by an extremely dedicated staff, and many authors coming to give talks about their work. It has been a place of meetings and information exchange, and that increasingly rare thing: an informal face-to-face gathering place where ideas can form and grow in discussion, where friendships and projects have begun. It has seen readings, spoken word performances, art and music – and has been one of the major centres of culture in the town for a fiercely loyal and surprisingly large group.

When I first heard that it was threatened with closure, I started a petition on 38 Degrees imploring the University of Portsmouth and Blackwell UK to think again. It got over a thousand signatures in one weekend. This bookshop was not only loved. It was needed.

As a casualty of the changing nature of information in the digital age, the demise of

Blackwell's Portsmouth can be seen in one light as a natural, even inevitable development.

That said, its corporate owners appear to have lacked the understanding and imagination to really make the shop work and flourish, given its unique role in the local writing scene.

Moreover, the shop's closure points to a broader problem: the disregard of large business entities for local communities. In its headlong rush to milk even more money from the venue, the University of Portsmouth has chosen to ignore the value Blackwell's added to its own reputation and the excellent service it provided its students. That will be to the University's lasting shame.

So, what really drove the closure of the bookshop?

The reality is that the idea of *university* died a death in Britain a generation ago. At least, the sort of institution I took my degree at in the early 1990s is dead. Even then, the idea of *university* was in the process of change, but there was still, in the slightly rarefied atmosphere of the philosophy department at York University where I studied, a sense of the value of learning a subject beyond its retail price conceived as a commodity. Back then, universities were, in fact, concerned with something far more important: culture.

But the role of the university as the custodian of culture is now defunct. And, if you are of the mind that art and culture are by-products of a successful economy, then you will take the accountant's view that Blackwell's Portsmouth's passing is the natural function of economic Darwinism.

If, however, you place a value on culture beyond that of numbers in a bank account, then the demise of Blackwell's is a belated weathercock for the way the wind has been blowing for the last thirty years.

Why, then, does this matter so much to me? Besides the personal support and purpose I found in the shop, it also strikes me that shutting a bookshop in a town with high levels of illiteracy is the wrong way to go. Now, only one retail bookshop is left in a city of 200,000 souls, and that is a generalist shop on Commercial Road that piles them high and sells the bestsellers cheap. That is one reason.

But I am also struck by an irony. Thanks to the work of John Pounds, a figure from the 1830s now largely forgotten, the right to a free education was born in Portsmouth. Pounds believed that education is for everyone, including the poorest – and especially those who could not pay for it. That was a noble cause which eventually spread to the offering of grants to all who made the grade, so they too could enjoy an elite education no matter what their personal finances. However, the political decision in 1998 to remove degree level grants has made education increasingly inaccessible and has enslaved a whole generation in massive debt; the result is that the inevitable logic of economics has led to education being at the vanguard of cultural decline. From a social good, education and culture have been demoted to, simply, *goods*.

It used to be the case that education and culture were regarded as something more broadly useful to society than being retailed as employability skills, important though they are. It was held that the very nature of what it is to be human could be broadened and made richer through an education that transmitted the values inherent to an enlightened culture, those of understanding others, of creative endeavour, of articulate questioning and challenging of orthodoxy. That used to be the role of the university. There was also a general belief that having people educated in this broader sense spread out as a good to society generally. This belief made the criteria for political and social decisions include aspects of life other than those dictated by basic economics. This view of education was the symptom of a holistic view of society and culture.

Now, however, pure right-wing economics are our master.

Some will argue that art and culture are by-products of civilisation – that our ancient forebears in the spare time between hunter-gathering needed something to do with their lives and so created art to while away their hours. Those people imagine that our ancestors, like us, came back from a hard day's hunting in the savannah and, in the absence of a flatscreen television, amused themselves by gawping at the Lascaux cave paintings – square-eyeing away the winter evenings for 10,000 years until their successors could eventually come up with Netflix.

This reductionist view of culture sees art and artistic endeavour as non-essential. It is the epiphenomenon of commerce. Artists and writers and poets and creators exist because they are supported by the real activity of life, which is all hard facts, and especially hard coin.

It is not a view I share. It seems obvious to me that the last thirty years has seen a general degradation of culture spearheaded by universities such as the one in Portsmouth. We are slowly going backward. We are devolving.

There's no doubt that hunting and gathering enabled early humans to work in co-operative groups; that it led to a particular type of social cohesion in the form of tribes; that it led to the necessity of building an understanding of the world around them – nor that all these are the foundations of modern life. No doubt, all these social behaviours are consequences of the activity that provided ancient humans with food and fire and safety – activities that would later be labelled economic.

But the ability to progress did not come from the act of hunting alone. Before the act of hunting in groups, someone had the idea that humans could work together, could find a way to trap an animal, could find food by hunting in packs. Every advance in human life is the result of an act of imagination, every advance comes from the visualisation and the discussion of ideas and possibilities. Yes, it is true that groups of creatures other than humans hunt in unison and do not paint cave walls or discuss Sartre over coffee, but none of those animals has the imagination to shape a flint or attach it to a spear, nor possess all the fine gradations and nuances in thinking and language that humans have, that have led to our rise over millennia. Ideas were born and passed from one generation to the next by culture and the spaces in which culture is transmitted, be they caves, temples – or bookshops.

That is why the sacred spaces of ancient cultures are covered in paintings, spells and words. That is why ancient civilisations such as the Babylonians sculpted creatures that were impossible in the real world, but which stepped straight from the imagination. It was not simple superstition expressed in the statues of ancient gods, it was not that artists and thinkers created fancies while the real business of the world continued despite them. Statues of ancient Gods and the rituals that surrounded them were central to the running of society, to civilisation's understanding of the world that was disseminated through temple rituals. Culture and the transmission of culture is humanity at its greatest. It has precedence over narrow economics.

And so we come back to Blackwell's Portsmouth.

There are arguments that the days of the book are long past. That with the coming of digitisation and with the ability of students to access material online, there is little need to produce books. Indeed, books are a terrible waste of resources, and the world is a greener place without all that wood pulp being converted. *Think of the environment*, we are enjoined. *Think of the planet.*

This misses the point of the rituals that occurred in this bookshop. Book launches, author talks, informal seminars, discussions, sharing, recommendations are more than *stock-in-trade*. Bookshops are not only purveyors of books, at least the good ones like Blackwell's in Portsmouth aren't. That goodwill could have been monetised, but the University wanted the site of the bookshop for another project. A British university didn't see the value in keeping its only functioning bookshop open. Let that thought sink in a while. Because it really is as simple as that.

Portsmouth's Blackwell's was a space where ideas could be disseminated beyond the economics-driven imperative of university finances. It drew people to it that were not connected to the university, and they met with students and lecturers and ideas were shared. Culture *happened* – spontaneously. Blackwell's was, in fact, a means of the transmission of culture just as the sacred spaces once were to our forebears. It was in its modest, modern way, a temple to civilisation.

Blackwell's wasn't only about commerce. It was about humanity in a wider sense. It was about standing up to the cost-benefit analysis view of life and saying, 'what we do, what we think, is vital because it is human, despite you' in the face of the machinery of bean-counting that pays lip service to such ideas, but sacrifices them to its own calculating god, Mammon.

My call, now, is that in its passing, we continue the rites enacted at Blackwell's Portsmouth, and work to preserve culture. That we do so, despite the decisions of businesses like Blackwell's UK, and the value-free institution that is the University of Portsmouth.

## Between Two Ports and the Hard Place

### Lewis Baglow (2015)

As a child, in the seventies, I would have nightmares about going to the City of Portsmouth. Not because I had heard tales of naval press-gangs bludgeoning people in the alleyways, or even the Battersea-esque landscape that spewed smoke like dragon's nostrils; it was because we always caught the ferry from Gosport. Oh, how I feared the flaky, green painted iron-bridge that descended onto a corrugated cowshed which floated on similarly coloured water. I shook at the sleeper-style flooring, requiring you to step over the gaps, as the waves underneath grabbed unsuspecting passengers by their sodden shoes and cowered at the clonk of the rust-laden vessels as they berthed portside, simultaneously jolting us crammed in cattle backwards and worst of all: buckled at the large, bulbous, Dalek-style rivets that held the whole structure together. I really wished that blue police box would appear and take me away! Now, forty years on and after extensive therapy, I have returned to face my childhood torment again; and make the crossing between two ports and the hard place.

Situated on the south coast of England, this vital ferry service operates between the quiet seafront town of Gosport and the busy docks lining the quays of Portsmouth (known locally as The Hard, due to its natural mooring shoreline). Its main ticketing office, based in Gosport, nestles amongst the coloured blooms of various trees and flower beds that encompass the Falklands Gardens; a memorial to the 1982 conflict in the South Atlantic; whilst from three convergence points, an endless stream of passengers filters through the waterfront complex, day and night, to cross the bridgeless expanse of water that separates them from the busy city.

It is the latter end of the rush hour ritual when I arrive at the ticket booth. The last stragglers of the insect-like commute soldier past me with their multi-trip passes in hand. Armies of black-suited banker ants rush to save the world, whilst the red secretarial varieties seductively tap along the pink pathways towards the jetty; careful to avoid the attentions of the green dockyard species that shamble around in groups. Along the promenade, bored pensioners begin to take their seats ready for today's performance of life goes by; filling the air with the unmistakeable seafront aromas of battered halibut and vinegar'd chips from the mid-morning special of the local fishery. Centre point and standing predominantly amongst the gardens, a two-tiered fountain begins to fill with the flow of disinterested unemployable; all scouring the base for loose change, in the hope of affording their next special brew.

In front of me, the queue quickly dwindles towards my destiny of facing a plastic window that's embedded into the side of the ticket building. Kennelled within, a well-travelled sea dog sits inside an uninteresting office; grunting his acknowledgment of the cupronickel-for-paper exchange of a boarding ticket. Now three pounds lighter, I begin to feel the weight of expectation as I start to approach the entrance to my haunted past. The orifice of the jetty looms menacingly, causing me to pause briefly as I become distracted by the seagulls circling around the blue backdrop above; screaming at the pigeons below who were now pestering the pensioners for their carbohydritic scraps; all as dark diesel clouds plume across the sky from the main bus terminal next door.

To my surprise, the old pontoon bridge of my childhood has now gone, replaced in 2011 with a new sleeker model, along with the Rolls-Royce of corrugated cowsheds; a futuristic design reminiscent of a Starbase rather than Homebase. It shows a twenty first century jump into a new millennia, from a ferry service that has operated for more than 400 years; making it one of the oldest running services still in operation within the United Kingdom. Today's lunar cycle has presented me with the lowest of tides; leaving me to teeter on the edge of a 300-degree incline to the berthing bay below. Through large glass panels either side, I torment the subdued tide with my dry shoes as I begin my descent into the depths of hell. With an unhelpful nudge of nature's gravity, I am forced to partake in a Naomi Campbell fall-style walk down the steep gradient; as semi-mounted cyclists freewheel past me with smug grins. With my boneage intact, I successfully make it onto the floating jetty and proceed to recover on the plastic 'bus stop-style' seating that runs along the edge of the interior.

Through the large windowed panelling that surrounds me, as well as the obligatory advertising posters, I watch as two ferries interchange with each other on their voyage to each respective pontoon; jostling for position amongst the bustling crowd of yacht masts swaying within the moorings of the numerous marinas that line the shores. Beneath my feet, the pontoon creaks and moans as it purposely buckles over the contours of lapping waves; creating a false sense of alcoholic intoxication that would benefit any weekend reveller looking for a cheap night out. Inside the terminal, a myriad of shoppers and students have gathered; patiently rocking as our designated vessel begins to manoeuvre into its docking position alongside us. With a ten knot and 200-ton jolt, the ferry grinds along the edge of the pontoon; squaring up to two sliding doors that allow access on and off the vessel. The waiting herd all take a sideways step from the resulting knock-on from the berthing ferry, which amuses me greatly; not just from the recollection of a childhood memory that lives on to this day, but from how I wished I had a banjo to facilitate the involuntary barn dance that ensued with each docking. With a quick lasso of the mooring ropes around the necks of the bollards from the ship's hands, this rodeo was ready to get under way.

The castered rumble of the sliding doors resonates throughout the corrugated structure, as the cattle market shuffles itself into position by the embarkation point. Fenced off by metal railings, the stampeding departees begin their race to the summit of the calamitous catwalk that ominously awaits them; as through the jostle ahead of me, the call of 'Watch your step, please!' brings flashback feelings of the trepidation I would feel as a youngster. Caught in the inescapable forward momentum, I squeeze through the waiting doorway; until I pause briefly at the see-sawing craft before me. Timing the motion of the bobbing ledge, I step clumsily aboard; mimicking the actions of a child's first experience of a department store escalator.

Now on board, the smug cyclists line in an orderly fashion amongst the miniature roll-on, roll-off surroundings of the welded interior. Rows of coach-style seating face the bow viewing area whilst through a doorway opposite; the train-carriage layout of tabled seats offers the ambience of a side-street café full of coffee breaking shoppers. A set of ladder-like stairs led me up to an open-aired deck; where I take a seat upon one of the wooden-strutted life rafts that sit neatly between two large funnels. To my relief, a red ant taps seductively to join me on my potential desert island; 'Well, at least if we sink,' I chuckle to myself, 'we'll be amongst the first to be evacuated, what with red ants and children and all that.' The pontoon doors slide again with thunderous closure, leaving the breathless disappointed to curse their misfortune and wasted last-minute dash; as the strangulated bollards gasp air again, allowing us to depart on our five-minute voyage.

A kick of the dual-rotored engine lathers up a frenzied whitewash of piranha-snapping bubbling; inviting the children on-board to clamber along the railings and marvel at the underwater agitation that rumbles around us. Deep vibrations begin to resonate through the seat up to my shoulders and, with a roar of dark plumage above me, we slide away from the pontoon. The pushed momentum allows the engines to quieten to a buzz; massaging me around the neck line as I squint at the skyline dominance of the Emirate sponsored Spinnaker Tower, Portsmouth's very own scaled-down Burj Al Arab. With arms leaned back, and legs stretched forward, I smile at the warmth against my closed eyelids; savouring in the tranquillity of being water-bound. Gone are the day-to-day rumblings of the road tearing traffic; replaced by the propelled rolling of the Isle of Wight hovercraft on the outskirts of the harbour mouth, the only service of its kind within the UK. Quirky honks and hoots randomly resonate from the various seafaring vessels that float freely along the lane-less spaghetti junctions. Calming slurps of lapped water within our wake sound gently amongst the calls of the gliding gulls as they dive briefly; disturbing the whiting schools that glisten with the twinkle of a thousand waved-crests. I must have relaxed a bit too much, as my seductive seating partner spoke softly: 'It's lovely on here isn't it?'

'Yes, it is,' I replied, revelling in my own dystopia, 'It's very relaxing.'

'It is. I love coming home on the ferry, it's so peaceful.'

I daren't ask where she had been. It was mid-morning and she was wearing the brightest of reds. I just smiled a response as the ferry swung around; manoeuvring itself alongside the pontoon that sat under the shadow of Portsmouth's piece of Dubai.

The exit of the stairwell was already blocked by the other passengers waiting to disembark. As we swung sideways, I gripped the cold metallic banisters with both hands as everyone skipped forward a step at the impending nudge of the docking hull. I managed to join the slow shuffle towards the bottlenecked gates; before stepping out onto a pontoon that was straight out of the 1970s. I didn't have time to panic at the onslaught of the oncoming inclination that had returned to haunt me; another forced momentum saw us bundled up the crumbling causeway, past the derelict ticket office and onto the concrete promenade of the Hard.

As the crowds dispersed, I was slapped with the eye watering drift of fried onion; emanating from a small greased-spoon shack that sat snugly by the top of the jetty. Alongside me, the shrill screech of mechanical metallic contact brought me a rude awakening from the tranquillity of a few moments earlier, as trains pulled in and out of the busy Portsmouth Harbour station. Trails of taxis rattled along the kerbsides that led to another diesel-infused bus terminal; all lined with the unfortunates of life enquiring after any change I may have. The Dubaian mirage had left me now, as under the towering masts of the historic warships that patriotically stand here, I felt a saddening at the destruction that the modern world had brought to this maritime setting. Thank heavens for those black-suited varieties for saving the world!

With a glance over my shoulder, I looked back with short-term nostalgia at the journey that I had just undertaken. The quiet town of Gosport seemed far more appealing from this side of the water; at least for my spare change, I would have been given some form of entertainment from the special brew crew rummaging in the fountain. Colourful blooms seemed redundant here, shadowed by the greys of structural decline with the crumbling facades of prehistoric plasterwork, but then this is a city after all; and my experience in similar monstrosities were no different to this. The haunting reminiscence from my childhood didn't seem so frightening now, compared to what I was facing.

An automatic knee-jerk took me back towards the direction of the jetty, smiling at the conquered demons as I made my way down the crooked inversion. With my return ticket, empathising with Charlie after he had found one of the Willy Wonka varieties, I joined the cattle drive which led to the next awaiting ferry. A sign over my head reads: 'It's shorter by water', the company's slogan; but as I board the vessel again, I couldn't help but wish that this urban escape jaunt would last just a little longer.

## How Can This Be? Waking Up in the Future

### Van Norris (2016)

*Author's note: This piece was written on the morning of 10 November 2016, upon waking up to the news of Donald Trump's election. Any amendments from the original publication on Star & Crescent have been merely to remove typos, extraneous material and to streamline the work for a different publishing setting.*

Increasingly, these days I feel like Jack Nicholson at the finale of Roman Polanksi's noir movie *Chinatown*. Bereft. Stunned. Faced with a jolt of uncomfortable reality. All I can honestly say to the current Western political climate is, 'How can this be?' (Polanski, 1974). Waking up to the news this morning that Donald Trump has been elected as the President of the United States feels like being trapped in the middle of a 1980s straight-to-DVD science-fiction film.

But I don't think Arnie is going to romp in here save the day. It's entirely feasible that he may well just audition for a place in Trump's cabinet instead. Yes, it feels like I can only process the world through film quotes these days, like some middle-aged, raddled, Portsmouth version of 'Abed' from *Community* (NBC 2009-2015).

So, what follows here are just my rambling thoughts. This is merely stuff that I had to get out of my head, so please excuse the odd lapse and disjointed phrase. It's always better 'out' than 'in' (as I always tell anyone who will listen).

Since Trump's surreal run for office began in June 2015, terabytes of information about the man have been passed around the internet. And over this past year we have witnessed a campaign like nothing any of us have ever seen (and in many ways hope to never see again). It has been like watching the very political system being dismantled and rendered as absurd before our very eyes.

As Trump seems to be the very embodiment of that curious phenomenon that clouds the populist worldview that fears any progressive, cautionary or (in truth) intelligent, rational narrative. He is a soundbite in human form. That a candidate can openly lie, blatantly contradict himself (within hours of each statement), survive a litany of highly credible accusations of sexual abuse, be openly racist, disablist, sexist and confrontational and aggressive to anyone who holds a different view to him is simply astounding. The demolition of political language and discourse alone has been staggering. And I was appalled at George Bush Jr.

Tellingly, as ex-*Daily Show* presenter, Jon Stewart, says, the current President can't even be left in charge of his own Twitter account without coming across like a thin-skinned, sulky, chivvying frat boy (see bibliography below). And one does wonder that, if Trump was to interview himself on his own show for the job of 'President', then he'd probably turn himself down on the basis of being temperamentally unsuitable for the role. But then, of course, he would quietly offer himself a post in the PR department once the cameras have been turned off, 'liking the cut of his jib'.

Donald Trump's major skill (quite evidently) is sales. Whether this translates to the stamina and focus required to be POTUS is another issue. This skill is what cemented his oddly untarnished reputation in the early 1980s, when he was central to the gentrification of New York. This is also the prime narrative that has informed his ongoing television show, *The Apprentice* (NBC 2003 – to date). As a businessman who inherited a vast family fortune and whose business interests have been declared bankrupt six times, now, seemingly, Trump is one of the few people able to somehow circumnavigate 'truth' and 'fact' and is in the position where he is able to self-perpetuate his own myth, a story built on narratives of 'success' and 'dominance'. Indeed, 'myth' seems to be the key word here. So apparently disconnected are we now today, we are more prepared to believe in myths now than we do in 'truth'.

The Brexit vote in June of this year (2016) has been cited, of course, as a parallel with the US election. Whereby the unexpected happened, the 'unthinkable'. Where the masses spoke in a voice that the 'liberal media elites' were either uninterested in listening to, or were simply incapable of deciphering with any clarity and projection. That campaign was helpfully summed up by the post-factual Michael Gove, (who of course was on the winning side), as the pinpoint where the populace had supposedly rejected expert opinion. A campaign where the voting public had seemingly become disillusioned with information and informed opinion.

This is a curious point for anyone to consider who has argued online with a rabid polemic pulling fragmented, unsourced statistics from the air to settle a 'lively debate' about immigration (this one could be the premise for another blog maybe). So yes, the hitherto 'silent' American majority appears to be afflicted with a similar dissatisfaction with the political system to ourselves. Sadly, they have followed suit and used a key vote as a howl of indignation and as a protest statement, rather than a constructive, ideological position. The 'myth' of the neoliberalism project is rejected, but not engaged with in terms of any lucidity or indeed within any credible scheme of genuine problem-solving. Throwing the toys out of the pram is a start, maybe, but not a solution.

So how did we get here? For me, many cultural shifts have been aligning over the last twenty years. As a lecturer in this area, it is understandable that I would feel that the institutional 'meeja' do have to take a major responsibility here. Certainly, as Danielle S. Allen noted, the perpetration of 'The Donald' as an easily transmissible construct, ideally suited to media coverage – and endlessly reconstituted and remixed in memes and status headings – has embedded him as a cultural force of unshakeable power (cited by Kristof, 2016).

'All publicity is good publicity' goes the cliché and, my God, has Trump proved that one right to the power of ten. As much as the media claim to hate him, he is a reliable fountain of endless quotes and outrage that actually has opened up that divide between the views of those in power and the views of the everyday person on the street. He is the end result of a self-serving media institution that has devalued political debate and intellectual thought, and this streamlining, highly mediated process has willingly reduced ideology to 'personality' and not 'policy'.

Remember, you never heard David Cameron talk about what Conservative ideology *really* is, as he probably would have lost loads of votes if he had. Nigel Farage (through his association with Trump, may become one of the most powerful brokers in the world) recognised this point entirely. Just tell a simple lie, tell it often and be 'a bit of a cheeky character' while you do it and you'll cut through the chatter. We've heard that before though, haven't we, back in the late 1930s...? (I bet, in retrospect, Nick Griffin wishes he'd been down the pub with a cameraman by his side bit more often).

For me, the big narrative underpinning the success of characters like Trump is social networking. When Andrew Keen prophetically warned us all about the dangers of letting the 'monkeys run the internet' (as he put it), there was undoubtedly some uncomfortable truth residing in that polemic on the death of the 'expert'. Albeit perhaps not exactly in the way that he predicted (Keen, 2005, pp. 2-3). For sure, the role and nature of 'gatekeepers' has shifted and this concept has become more fluid and more complex and difficult to assess. Today, I genuinely do feel that we're in a state of flux, as our (now global) social sphere still struggles to deal with the sudden mass of confusing and contradictory information, opinion, polemic and representation that typifies our online world, in direct contrast to the pre-digital climate. We are in a painful transition period between social and philosophical states. Hopefully this will be one we can negotiate before, as comedian Frankie Boyle said earlier today: 'Trump falls face first onto the nuclear button.' (2016).

Certainly, as stated earlier, Trump functions as the perfect social network icon. Simplistic, immediate, open to any reconstitution that can stand any Photoshopped interpretation and yet still retain shape and instant recognition. He is a 'surface', a component in our online world, a funnel for comment and for self-reflection and, as has become apparent this morning, for self-definition.

Part of this transition between states i.e. the pre-social networking and a world where this new medium has been fully quantified and rationalised into human existence, is that we have now become aware of our world and its workings in ways that we could never have been prepared for. The other profound issue that has undoubtedly affected our individual lives is that we have become face-to-face with the sheer chaos, the overwhelmingly fragmented nature and day-to-day injustice of our world.

This tidal wave of information is also filtered through media organisations struggling to find a voice and a market position in this fast-paced traffic of images, opinion and pseudo-events. And this conflicting, highly intense, sometimes confusing and occasionally frightening view of our global hive-mind is beamed straight into our palms, daily, minute-by-minute. Shifting. Colourful. Maddening. Contradictory. Inspirational. Immediate. Trump is ideally suited to this climate. His speeches read like an *Independent* news feed or the Twitter ramblings of a lunatic, i.e. fragmented, sensationalist and often misleading and inaccurate. (Remember, up until fairly recently Trump openly thought that the Republican electorate was a gullible enough resource to openly exploit and that his favourite politician was Bill Clinton – or was this 'fake news'?) (Lerner, 2015).

Understandably, perhaps, when faced with such an overwhelming state of information overload inevitably many retreat into nostalgia and comforting, often-imagined certainties, (à la Frederic Jameson's ideas on the endgame of postmodern culture itself) (1991). The Trumpian cry to 'Make America Great Again' certainly suggests this inward-looking trajectory underpins most political opinion these days.

Through social networking we have all been experiencing and hearing oppositional political voices on a daily basis in an intense, highly focused barrage of short, barking slogans. Many coming to this landscape are hearing views that they either don't like, don't understand or find too challenging to engage with (and this is on *both* sides of the political spectrum, remember). Ideas appear with such speed that we barely have time to digest them and work through, before yet another screams in our face. If you're working a 'zero hours' contract, have a family, doing long shifts at work or simply overwhelmed in this increasingly nasty post-economic crash climate then who honestly has the time to *think*? Who has the time and capacity to be idealistic? If you're still struggling to eat in this work setting, the rejection of this perceived 'liberal consensus' may seem particularly hypocritical. Especially when it comes from 'an elite'. Indeed, I always have to remind myself that just because I'm hearing an opinion I don't agree with online, doesn't mean that that's *all* there is out there. So potent and so distorting can our perceptions of this sphere of commentary be.

The social networking environment, as we know, is all about instantaneous and boiled-down commentary. It is perhaps understandable when the only political dialogue that holds any traction today is the simplistic, the reactionary. You can't really boil down a nuanced debate to 140 characters (and God knows I've tried), all you can do is shout and rage and reach out to similar voices – which does rather confirm Adam Curtis' view of Twitter as a 'hollow, conservative echo chamber' whereby we only reach out and include in our networks those who hold views similar to ourselves (cited by Ronson, 2015).

An issue that intersects with this phenomenon (and I think most profoundly here), is that we are now experiencing an organised rejection of 'political correctness' by a generation who don't seem to know what the term actually *means* as a mechanism and are aware at what purposes it actually served in the 1980s into the 1990s as an all-important societal mechanism to deal with social injustice and issues of reduction around race, gender and sexual orientation. It is, and always was, an ideal rather than a political party or fixed agenda.

Today's conception is informed by a *distortion* of that very positive idea, as the term now seems to embody dialogues of constriction, reaction and over-sensitivity. Rather than attack PC, it might be more prudent to deconstruct the true landscape of litigation, fear, ignorance and half-formed and inconsistent views on personal space that this current refraction of that term is in fact *really* addressing in today's strange extension of that original (very worthy) concept. What we're witnessing here is of course an intense connection to a state of individualism. This is all about ourselves and separation. Isolating and insulating ourselves from a scary life-out-there that we experience through photographs and news feed hook-lines. An idea too easily twisted into a condemnation of anyone who has a progressive bent. But one that has undoubtedly shifted the nature of our online value system.

The profound role social networking has played in the rise of the demagogue also hinges on another important factor. Charlie Brooker's excellent *Black Mirror* (currently on Netflix) addressed this phenomenon in the conclusion to his episode 'Nosedive' (2016). For as we hide behind avatars and as we become more and more socially atomised and distant from each other, as we are freed from the constrictions and almost sociopathic need to be 'liked' and 'approved' in our daily lives, as we seek to attain 'success', views and ideas that could never have been expressed in open conversation in past decades are aired in this removed, unforgiving and unfiltered space on a regular basis. Opinions that would never have been offered in daily conversation, for fear of instant vilification, are expressed so often that they have been taken for a 'norm' and as a signifier for 'reality'. Rather than as part of a rational, nuanced, interactional discussion between two people.

This has created an odd parallel consensus, one that has increasingly become divorced from empathy whereby our *real* lives have been subsumed by our internal, *online* lives. We are now face-to-face with ourselves as a people and our own darkest thoughts. The Twittersphere has revealed our own collective psyche in its glory and in its ugliness. We are now privy to the foaming instant reactive rages of the mentally tormented, the disassociated, the afraid, the isolated, the uninformed, the polemics and their opinions, that used to be hidden or contained behind closed doors. As overwhelming and potent as they are, they now hold equal prominence with the informed, the adjusted, the expert, the idealist and the positivist. This flattening out process is maybe what Keen (perhaps hysterically) warned us about in 2005, but it has brought into being an oddly contradictory climate that shrieks and howls over outrages about racism and sexism but then does little to actually go out in the real world and do anything meaningful about it.

In truth, Trump is the manifestation of Adam Curtis's ideas on individualised protest (2011). Whereby people rally round for a brief glorious moment, revelling in the chance to overturn the system and make themselves 'heard'. They complain, they stamp their feet, they demand 'change' and they then oust the focal point of their rage. In this case it's the 'political and liberal elites'. Soon, I have no doubt, it will be intellectuals, academics and anyone who seems a bit 'untrustworthy'. After that? Who knows?

After this moment of catharsis, the same system reassembles itself but becomes better equipped to deal with resistance and challenge. Real change comes in increments. Certainly, the kind of change necessary to really make a difference that doesn't mean people get hurt in large numbers. Change doesn't happen from pressing a button to vote for your favourite personality. It doesn't come through a Twitter post. It comes through engaging with your surroundings, with your system and indeed with ideology and a worldview that extends beyond yourself and your immediate needs. Without constructive thought we get Trump. We get reaction and no real solution. As Alexei Sayle said in interview with the comedian Stewart Lee about his disillusionment with politics, sadly the Right don't keep making the same mistakes the Left do (2015). He was very, *very* right there.

It may well be that Donald Trump signifies this difficult transition period between pre-social networking and a world more at ease with the concept, as we struggle to deal with the complexity of our world and to shape a globalised culture that is still, remember, in its inter-connected infancy. It could well be this is a momentary reaction and that the generation that follows will be much more adjusted to negotiate the tidal wave of information that we now have to deal with on a daily basis.

Although, as one of the 'liberal elites' typing away on my yacht, I'm now away to watch the rest of *Black Mirror*. So, of course, you really can't believe a word I say.

## The Next Station Is

## Richard Williams (2017)

Portsmouth and Southsea then Fratton and Hilsea,
clattering over the creek to the points at Cosham
west to Southampton, Salisbury and Cardiff,
east to Brighton, north to Waterloo.

And you will catch your breath in her reflection,
watching the world from a window seat,
as seasons concertina in ripening fields.
Commuter belt villages and old market towns,
reels of film on a cutting room floor;
are the scenes we keep the ones we'd choose?

And she will be returning here in your arms,
like yawning workers on the stopping train
memories slurring as carriages sway,
past Bowlplex, Vue and the lipstick tower.

Morning always loops home to this place.
dawn into day into dusk into night.
A circle aching still to be filled
with children's laughter like marker pens.
Love and hope in permanent ink;
this city by the sea and all that you need.

## The Liberty Wars

## Maddie Wallace (2018)

Thank you. Thank you. I was honoured to be asked to speak today at such an important service. The work we are all doing in rebuilding our lives is still an ongoing struggle. Today we remember those who aren't here anymore. The following are some of the letters my mother wrote to my sister Hannah during the siege.

21 March 2023

Dear Hannah,

I'm still going to keep writing these in the hope that you are alive, and that the battle in Southampton didn't affect your area too much. I've been so worried because your halls are right in the middle of town, and all I've heard is that a lot of the city centre was hit hard.

It's Sam's birthday today, he's seventeen. I still haven't seen either of your brothers, it's been over three months, but I did speak to Zach last week on the radio. I can't leave it on for long though, it's too risky. It seems like only yesterday that your birthdays were spent surrounded by balloons and banners, with a pile of presents on the dining room table for when you woke up. The exotic, bittersweet smell of freshly brewed coffee to keep me awake, because I always left the decorating to the last minute the night before. The excitement of siblings enjoying each other's birthday, rushing to give presents before school. Pancakes and blueberries for breakfast. It also feels like a lifetime ago. The only present I want now is for this siege to be over.

It didn't seem that bad to begin with. The conveys rolled in; first the reconnaissance and patrol vehicles, then the tanks, the artillery, the heavy transporters with their grumbling engines and huge rumbling tyres almost as tall as me. Lots of foot soldiers – most were bedraggled and tired. We watched them on Goldsmith Avenue. Some people were cheering, but many stood quietly like us, absorbing the sight and sound of what was left of the British Army as they brought their leaders to the last bit of safety left; Portsmouth.

There wasn't a great deal of change to begin with. It was late spring, almost a year ago, warm with the smell of cherry blossom along the common. Locals mixed with the soldiers who set up camp in various residential areas. They favoured parks and schools, being amongst the residents for protection. There were even sunny days on the common at first, although muted. No one had meat for a barbecue and the alcohol was dry before they even arrived. What I'd give for a glass of Campo Viejo! I expect it will be years before Spain is producing wine again.

I worry so much about the boys, but I'm proud of them too. They said they needed to join in the fight, to help free us. I'd rather they were here so I know they're safe, but I know how much the resistance needs people. I'd have volunteered if I didn't have Eve to look after, but I do my bit with reconnaissance of the school and reporting suspicious activity on the radio. I have to keep it hidden in the old coal chute in the cellar, behind a loose brick. That's where I keep these letters too. They'd shoot me if they found them. Eve should be around the corner playing in the park like you guys were at her age, not stuck in a damp cellar every day. The park is a Loyalist campsite now.

Love Mum x


30 March 2023

Dear Hannah,

I'm so sorry to have to tell you but the dog died this morning. I can't even feel pain any more. Eve cried for hours, but I feel as though if I cry I might die. I considered eating her, but in the end, we buried her in the garden. She was so old and thin it wasn't worth it. Still no word from the boys. I heard from a man in the food distribution centre that the fighting is almost to the hill now. They're saying if the forts fall, the siege will be over. I hope it's true.

A soldier at the centre stared at Eve in a way that made me want to stab him. Too long with his eyes on her face, leering at her swelling chest. I've told her she can't go out any more. She doesn't want me to go alone, but she's growing up, and I can't risk it. We all know what they did to the women at Milton Cross food centre. It's happening all the time now. Nowhere is safe.

All my love Mum x

1 April 2023

Dear Hannah,
We are all fools. Who knew that World War III would mean civil war on a global level? All that worry about the superpowers, and the real fight was within. I have no more to say, I am drunk with the idiocy of it all.

6 April 2023

Dear Hannah,
You'll never believe it – Zachery came!
He looks so thin, but strong too. And different, more grown up. I wish you could see him, but I'm glad you're not here. I pray you are OK.
He didn't stay long, he said he was moving from safe house to safe house but didn't want to risk us being searched when he was here. He bought vegetable seeds! He's seen Sam, they were together up until last week in Hilsea. He wouldn't say much, he didn't want to give me knowledge that could be tortured out of me, but they were involved in the attack on Gunwharf last weekend. We could hear the gunfire and we went out in the garden after dark and could see the orange glow to the west where the tower was burning. The air was filled with the smell of thick smoke and cordite for two days.
The P.A.E have tried not to shell too much of the city's infrastructure so it can still function after the war is over, so it was a battle fought mostly on foot by the resistance. He said they managed to land soldiers on Eastney beach at night, but not as many as they could have done with. The Loyalists have left Gunwharf now though. The resistance managed to call in a direct artillery hit on their base in the underground carpark. I heard they rounded up and killed all the women and children who had been living in the John Pounds Centre for that.
It was so strange when it all started. So surreal. It all seemed to escalate so quickly after the government's involvement with Russia over the Brexit vote became clear. When Scotland seceded, and little pockets of what they called 'rioting' started in the bigger cities, it just didn't seem real, did it? All that sabre rattling, and then the fighting started on the borders. We still had TV then, and electricity, although both were sporadic. The internet went early on of course. To stop the

rebels coordinating. That was not long before we last saw you. It took almost a year for the fighting to start here. It trickled down the country from the Scottish border like shifting sands. Even when London was involved it was all still very normal, was it like that in Southampton too? The schools were still open for quite some time. I remember hoping the fighting would miss us just like the rain sometimes does, blowing inland over Portsdown Hill, with us a little island oasis.

I hugged Zachary so tightly when he left. I'm torn between pride that he is fighting to free us, and terror that he'll die.

Love Mum x


9 April 2023


Dear Hannah,

We woke up in the night to shelling, and it's still going on. It's terrifying. Great thundering booms, one after another after another. When it started Eve and I both jumped up and tried to light a candle, but the thick dust falling from the brickwork with each explosion smothered it. We used the torch for a while, taking it in turns to wind it up. Then we just lay there in the dark, holding tightly to each other, coughing as debris from the ceiling and the hall floor smattered onto us in convulsive gasps, as if the house was groaning with disgust. We must have fallen asleep, because I dreamt of you as a little girl, and that time we went on holiday to Spain with Dad, before the boys were born.

I woke up wishing he was still alive, but then I realised the narrow strip of window to the side path above the cellar was letting in daylight, and Eve and I were both ashen grey and thick with dust. We looked like we'd walked out of a volcanic eruption.

I wonder how history will look at all this. What was the final straw? History is a funny business, it's subjective even though it lays claim to being objective. If the Loyalists had held London and pushed the P.A.E. back, and then maybe won, how would they tell it all? No doubt it would all be about Corbyn inciting violence. They'd probably forget it was the far right who started it all when Scotland seceded. They'd leave out that Corbyn was calling for peace and trying to stop the violence. They'd say he died a traitor and that Tommy Robinson was a martyr.

Miss you so much. Love Mum x

17 April 2023

Dear Hannah,

I think it will be over soon, the shelling has been continuous for over a week. It must be the final push. The smoke from the hill is black where they are fighting for the forts.

I remember once trying to explain to a friend that the forts were originally designed to protect the city from an attack from behind Portsdown Hill. The Victorians were worried Napoleon would try and land his forces further down the coast and march inland to take Portsmouth from on top of the hill. Ironically, that's now what's happening, but instead of Napoleon, it's King William and the P.A.E. Although he doesn't call himself King anymore. Who would want to be King these days? If we're all going to live harmoniously we can't have monarchs. The days of the elite are over. Except in Portsmouth. They still reign here.

I haven't been out today, it's not safe anymore. The food distribution centres are all closed now, although when I went out to try and find wood for a fire yesterday I bumped into Lucy. You remember, from round the corner? Emma's mum? She was looking for wood too, and she told me that the Loyalists have been going house to house over in Copnor and rounding up anyone they can find. No one knows where they're taking them.

I'm not going out anymore. Eve and I have some onions and potatoes left, but I daren't light a fire now, not if they're doing to house to house searches.

I love you, I hope you are OK. Love Mum x

That was her last letter.

The following day Loyalist soldiers came in trucks and started banging on doors. We'd heard the noise of vehicles in the road, and then gunfire, so we went upstairs and peaked out the front through the gap in the boarding over the lounge window. They were kicking down doors and raiding the houses, dragging people out by their hair. Any men were being shot on the spot, and they were putting the women and children on trucks. My mother rushed us down to the cellar and hid me at the back of the old coal chute under the chair. My brothers had made a fake wall to put underneath it, so from a distance it looked like there nothing there. I was curled up behind the pretend wall, hugging my knees, doing my breathing exercises so I wouldn't panic. We'd drilled for this; over and over.

I heard them come in. I heard one of them shout at my mother. She went compliantly – I know it was to protect me – I heard them lead her up the stairs. I held my breath as gritty footsteps came closer, down the coal corridor, towards the chute. Shards of torchlight were creeping towards me past the fake wall, which was really only a painting on plywood. My mother and brothers had said it was convincing from a distance, but the soldier was close. My ears felt like they were full of blood, –pulsing. So that I couldn't tell if I was hearing my own pulse or that of the ocean.

There was a shout from above, and a roar from my mother so primal I wet myself. The soldier in the coal chute turned and ran, I heard his footsteps pounding up the cellar stairs towards the commotion going on above my head in the hall. One of the survivors of that day said it took five of them to drag her out, and she took three of them down before they shot her. When we were liberated three days later, they found that the Loyalists had burned hundreds of bodies in what was left of the football stadium. We think that's what happened to her.

Never before in all of human history has so much damage been done to so many by so few. As we commemorate all those lives lost ten years ago, may that war – and all the other uprisings that happened around the world at that time – serve to remind us that left unchecked, human nature can lead towards selfishness, repression, greed and violence.

Two billion brothers and sisters across the world gave their lives that we may all be free of the tyranny of leadership and corruption. I stand here today with my brothers and my sister to remember our mother, and all those we lost in Portsmouth, at our new Liberty Memorial. We must never forget their sacrifice.

## Howling at the Coffee Cup (or One Man's Love for Eastney Beach)

### Andrew Larder (2018)

Poet John Masefield wrote, 'I must go down to the sea again, to the lonely sea and the sky.' I have similar feelings; I'm addicted to walking along Eastney beach.

My relationship with this stretch of Southsea was born from necessity rather than choice. I live approximately two miles away from the seafront with my wife and two teenage children, and College Park is only two minutes' walk from my house. When we inherited a rescue dog I needed to find somewhere different to walk him because during wet weather he was slowly bringing the park into our house, muddy lump by muddy lump.

My addiction is not part of a midlife crisis, though it may be part of a mature mental 'kerfuffle' over my previous perceptions of the beach. In times of distress, the Bible mentions a 'great wailing' or 'gnashing of teeth'; but at my age and with my teeth 'gnashing' seems foolhardy, and 'wailing' seems an inadequate description. Besides, this text includes a dog, so 'howling 'seems more appropriate.

In this story, there will be howls, some howling, and probably a few howlers. Please note that howls can be induced by pain, grief or laughter.

Howl No 1

When summer is over and you realise the opportunity to develop the perfect beach body – complete with a six-pack and tan – is gone, it's tempting to pretend it's still warm. On a day closer to October than August, it's easy to misjudge the strength of the sun or the wind chill factor and wear shorts only to discover too late that you are now dressed entirely inappropriately for the beach. Blue lips with matching knees and a stomach resembling less a six-pack and more a badly folded cardigan.

Why am I at the beach in shorts in bad weather?

I never wanted a dog. As a married man, father of two teenagers and Pompey season ticket holder, I only have so much love to spare.

By an act of fate and much guilt-tripping by my children, we ended up with a dog. I shall call him Dog. I refuse to use his given name for reasons that will become apparent later.

Before accepting Dog into our house, I stated that responsibilities would be shared equally amongst our family. With this rule in place, I now exercise the dog, feed the dog and pay any vet bills.

And that's how I ended up at badly dressed for the beach. Regular walks keep him calm and more importantly quiet at night.

Howl No 2

I've spent most of my life in Portsmouth but when I meet people from other parts of the country they're often baffled my family have no connections to the Royal Navy, that I do not sail, nor fish, and I rarely swim in the sea.

My father was a Yorkshireman. He would take my mother, my sisters and I to Eastney Beach every Sunday morning during the summer. I have fond memories of sausage sandwiches, tea brewed on a little camping stove, splashing in the sea and playing football on the patchy grass; my lightweight, black and white ball often blown off course or backwards by the strong winds.

If all this sounds idyllic, it was - except for one small thing.   The French philosopher Jean Paul Sartre famously said, 'Hell is other people.' I often thought that Sartre might be a Yorkshireman as my Father shared his outlook. To 'avoid the crowds 'and 'find a parking spot' we often left our house at 6am and were home by 10am.

My Dad loved Eastney Beach. While I craved building sandcastles, he adored the shingle because 'you don't get grit in your bits.'

Initially, my trunks were far too big but as the years passed, they became extremely snug. Dad's trunks were faded blue cotton shorts, lined with nylon netting, and also used for decorating and gardening. They warranted their own sub section in the Public Order Act. Splattered on the front with flecks of white paint with a brown stain on the rear left by some tar he had sat in. To make things worse the first time he met my beloved wife to be, he had been gardening, the netting had stretched and become slack. When he sat down a single saggy testicle popped out to greet her.

Howl No 3

The first impressions of Eastney beach might be of a bland stretch of shingle beach from South Parade Pier to the mouth of Langstone

Harbour. However, hours spent pacing up and down this stretch of the seafront have made me realise Eastney beach holds many secrets.

Take time to walk down to the water's edge. The outgoing tide reveals sandy stretches teeming with the life usually concealed beneath the waves. The first time I saw vibrant green and red seaweed was here at Eastney beach. Razorfish, cuttlefish, starfish and jellyfish are often to be found, washed up and abandoned by nature. As a fellow creature, you would think Dog would have more respect, but he does not. Instead, Dog has a strict sniff, prod, and piddle policy.

Some days the beach is beautiful, others like a brutal battlefield of mutilated crabs in various stages of decomposition, and crows - not seagulls - feasting on the dead.

Dog has a favourite tasty snack. Looking like a cross between a ball of soggy rice crispies and yellow bubble wrap, his doggy delicacy of choice is a clump of whelk's eggs. Whelks are odd creatures. When fully formed they are snails that glide along hoovering decaying detritus from the seabed. Each rice crispy capsule can contain hundreds of eggs. The first whelk to hatch will eat the rest of their siblings: a disturbing tale of gastropod cannibalism that betrays the Disney vision of the circle of life.

Public information bards adorn the seafront giving examples of the range of flora and fauna to be found. Many have intriguing names: the Nottingham Catchfly, Haresfoot Clover and the Yellow Horned Poppy. Others have self-explanatory names, such as Sea Beet, Sea Holly and Sea Kale. The plants burrow past the stones and sand to take root, surviving winds, high and low temperatures and salty sea air. The shingle is formed from flint that has broken away from the chalky Dorset Coast and this type of vegetated shingle is only found in North West Europe, New Zealand and Japan. The wonderous creations that live here, millions of years in the making, are now subjected to an insidious assault from plastic. By 2050, if we do not stop polluting the oceans, there will be more plastic than fish in the sea.

Howl No 4

Not quite the Solent Riviera or the Malibu of Southsea, development around Eastney has been limited and not without controversy. The Fraser Range site is the subject of a proposed housing development as I write, although some local nudists may object.

A duel cycle lane was introduced to preserve the life of cyclists. However, raised kerbs, high winds, and the many car occupants and pedestrians trying to traverse the road make the whole affair somewhat hazardous. I think the idea was devised by a road safety engineer who played a lot of *Frogger* in the eighties.

Historically the area is rich. The Royal Marines Barracks, slowly being sold off for housing, lost its museum in April 2018, and the fate of the infamous Yomper is unknown at the time of writing (a consultation was completed in February 2018). The interior and exterior are impressive but seem doomed to be sold off to property developers.

Eastney beach was where the 'Cockleshell Heroes' of World War Two trained. Five two-man canoes set off to paddle up the River Gironde, 75 miles into occupied France and sabotage ships in the docks with limpet mines. Churchill claimed their actions shortened the war by six months.

A couple of years ago a café popped up on Eastney sea front. A few doubted the need for another coffee outlet, but the venue has been popular, bringing new visitors to the area. More broadly in Portsmouth and beyond, purveyors of quality hot beverages have enjoyed something of boom. In 2013 the UK spent some £730 million pounds on coffee and the market continues to expand. According to the British Coffee Association, the British drink 95 million cups a day.

Howl No 5

One evening in January I had to take Dog for a walk. It was only 5pm but already pitch black as I headed down to Eastney Beach, keen to try out Dog's recently purchased cheap illuminated glow collar. Walking away from the road I was struck at how quickly the darkness engulfed me. City lights to the rear, in front of me I could hear the waves but could barely make out their shape. In the distance, lights on the Isle of Wight and shipping lanes twinkled. I played blind man's bluff along the storm ridge and Dog trotted off. I carried on walking and then I saw Dog had stopped. I got closer and thought he had found something edible as he was standing still. A strong wind off the water built up and I realised that Dog had slipped his collar, which lay propped up against some seaweed. I kept calm and started to call Dog's name: once or twice in quick succession, then louder and longer. What if he had gone in for a swim, in the darkness he might get disorientated and start swimming towards Ryde illuminations or follow a banana boat back to Columbia.

I trudged towards the café, continuously calling, my shouting growing more desperate. Less shouting, more crying now, and tinged with panic, I was soon up by the café. The people inside were oblivious to my pain, and I hated them for sipping their flat whites and ignoring my plight. Bathed in the yellow light they looked like extras in a Denis Hopper painting.

I called out again and this time I threw my head back and the result was less a cry and more a howl. I looked across to the café, I could not hear them, so I was sure they could not hear me, but they had all stopped sipping and were staring at me. I marched around repeatedly calling his name. Why were they staring? Then I realised.

Dog's real name is Fudge. I was shouting 'Fudge' at the top of my voice. But they were inside and to these amateur lip readers I just looked like I was stomping about shouting a word that clearly started with an 'F' and a 'U'.

Everyone returned to their flat whites. After thirty minutes and on the verge of giving up, it was a huge relief when I found Fudge with a kind woman.

'He just came straight up to me and sat quietly.'

The lady obviously thought I was a hopeless dog owner. After she had gone I gave Fudge a good piece of my mind and then a dog biscuit because I am a hopeless dog owner.

That was my first and last beach walk in the dark.


Howl No 6

On Saturday mornings the Park Run thunders along the pavement, occasionally intersecting with triathletes in training. A steady stream of joggers in shorts, puffing and huffing along the promenade, nod in acknowledgement to wet-suited men and women heading towards the sea. If you must wear a rubber outfit to survive in the water that might be a clue that you are not supposed to be in the water. However, I have nothing but admiration for these dedicated enthusiasts as I stumble along with my cardigan belly and blue knees.

There is something for everyone on Eastney beach, even sci-fi geeks like myself: in 1971 episodes of the Dr Who adventure 'The Sea Devils' were filmed in this area.

These days I enjoy the beach all year round: its different colours reflected in the varying strength of sunlight. When the sea is a field of sparkling diamonds, the waves whoosh up and down the shingle and the only howl is the wind, I know I am lucky to have all this on my doorstep.

## 'Not Your Meeting': Flawed Democracy in the Council Chamber

### Shelagh Simmons (2016)

Public opinion on the Solent Combined Authority and the Arts Lodge at Victoria Park were swept aside at the Full Council Meeting on 11th October 2016, despite active community opposition and a complete failure by local politicians to demonstrate a meaningful public mandate for their decision-making.

But there was another issue on the agenda that day in which I had a personal interest: the state pension age (SPA) and the way its equalisation has been unfairly and cruelly implemented for women born in the 1950s. It is the subject of a major campaign I am involved with led by Women Against State Pension Inequality (WASPI), who recently announced plans to legally challenge the government on their pensions policy. We want fair transitional arrangements for thousands of women – including here in Portsmouth – who expected to receive their pensions at 60 but now have to wait up to another six years without proper notice and time to prepare for such a major change. Former Portsmouth MP Flick Drummond supported the campaign and was a founder member of an All Party Parliamentary Group lobbying the government to introduce transitional arrangements for women affected.

It's fair to say there is a lot of opposition to the plans.

Former Minister of State for Pensions, Baroness Ros Altmann, outlined strong concerns about the policy in her resignation letter to the Prime Minister in 2016. She stated that 'short-term political considerations, exacerbated by the EU referendum, have inhibited good policy-making' on pensions, and continued:

'I am not convinced the Government adequately addressed the hardship facing women who have had their state pension age increased at relatively short notice.'

Numerous councils – including Manchester, North Devon, Newcastle, Plymouth and Blackpool – joined the former pensions minister in her concerns and voted to support the WASPI campaign by writing to the Secretary of State on our behalf. In September 2016, the Isle of Wight Council joined them. A motion proposed by Labour

Councillor Geoff Lumley attracted cross-party support, and he said in a recent council meeting:

'We need to send a message to government that we care about the 1,500-2,000 Islanders this will affect.'

When the motion was raised on the Isle of Wight, Council Leader, Councillor Jonathan Bacon (independent), said he didn't understand why anyone wouldn't support it. He didn't have too far to come to find out.

11 October 2016 was an important day in the WASPI campaign as petitions signed by tens of thousands around the country were handed in to Parliament. It was particularly important for campaigners and residents when a similar motion – proposed and seconded by Liberal Democrat councillors – came before Full Council on the same day

It felt like an auspicious day for our motion - that is, until then Council Leader Donna Jones stood up and called for it to be kicked down the road to a scrutiny committee. Jones said postponing the debate would deliver 'a much fuller and thorough discussion than here at the Council, and actually, this isn't a local issue.'

She then explained that postponing the planned democratic debate was justified because the issue deserved full and thorough discussion, presumably why so many other councils across the country chose to debate it at similar meetings. In Portsmouth, the debate was tabled for a full council meeting and, until her surprise announcement that it should be delayed, was assumed to be taking place. All councillors were present (ensuring all wards and residents were fully represented), and interested residents and groups were present for the debate – some had submitted deputations. It was hard to understand the Leader's explanation that delaying the debate somehow better served local democracy.

Neither was her stated concern that state pensions are not 'a local government matter' any easier to understand, given the Full Council debate on leaving the EU that took place in March 2016.

State pensions is an issue affecting thousands of local women, as reported on Portsmouth North MP Flick Drummond's website:

'In Portsmouth South, according to the independent House of Commons Library, around 3,010 women are directly affected by the 2011 Pensions Act alone. 241 local residents signed the e-petition calling for transitional arrangements, which received almost 200,000 signatures nationwide.'

Given its local relevance, when Lib Dem councillors submitted the motion, the item was accepted for debate and placed on the agenda.

The City Solicitor, Michael Lawther, later confirmed that he considered it an appropriate item for inclusion. I submitted a written deputation to be included in the Council's considerations. Those of us waiting for the debate sat in the public gallery for over 4 hours, until past 6pm. All Conservative members voted in favour of the Leader's suggestion, which suggests there was some coordination of their vote in advance.

Having asked at the start of the Council meeting who was eligible to take part in the debate, why did the Leader then allow residents to sit and wait for 4 hours before announcing her intention to pull the item?

I was shocked to see the Leader's supporters included two of my own ward councillors, Conservatives Luke Stubbs and Jennie Brent (who also happens to be a victim of this policy). Both were fully aware of how important this matter is to me because I wrote to them about it.

In our correspondence on the issue, Councillor Stubbs complained about the lost value of his own private pension. While I have some sympathy, if you are a fan of the unfettered free market – as he is – you can hardly complain when it comes back to bite you. But this isn't about a private pension. It's about a contract between individuals and the state. The contract is that we work and contribute to the country in exchange for a small amount of dignity and security in our older years.

Many of the women affected by the changes to pensions have had no opportunity to build up their pension pots. They are totally reliant on their state pensions. And with the gender pay gap not projected to fully close for another 43 years, women continue to be disadvantaged.

Both my councillors witnessed my distress – and that of others in the public gallery – when they and fellow Conservatives decided to delay the debate. Despite my previous correspondence with them on the subject, neither subsequently approached me to explain their decision.

Shocked at the sudden revelation that they had waited for four hours to participate in local democracy for absolutely nothing, residents and campaigners – myself included – raised our voices in protest. In response, the Lord Mayor reprimanded us, stating that 'There's a democratic process,' something it might have been useful for him to remind his own Members.

The Lord Mayor then told us, 'Please leave the Chamber. If you don't leave the Chamber, I'm getting security.'

The decision to pull the debate was shocking to the public in the gallery, and the handling of it seemed strange and insensitive, to say the least. But why would the Leader have wanted to delay this particular debate?

Some might speculate that if the debate had gone ahead, it could have been embarrassing for the then Minister of State for Department of Work and Pensions, Penny Mordaunt, also MP for Portsmouth North. It could be seen as embarrassing to demonstrate a lack of support for the women's pensions policy in her own constituency on the very day an endless stream of petitions against the changes were being delivered to Parliament.

To those unfamiliar with the antics of our local politicians, the decision to postpone a debate may seem inconsequential, but for residents who regularly engage and participate in local politics, it was only the latest incident in a broader trend of behaviour towards residents, organisations and groups who criticise Council policy.

Other councils have supported local women's concerns about their future under the current pension plans. By contrast, Portsmouth City Council dismissed them and threatened us with the police when we protested.

While continuing to insist women's pensions aren't a local issue, Donna Jones later said she was actually 'hugely sympathetic' to our plight. This sympathy certainly wasn't evident to the public on the day of the meeting when, finding herself being challenged on her decision to delay the planned debate, she barked, 'We just need to go to the vote then, don't we?' The vote to postpone the debate was decided overwhelmingly by the Conservative voting in favour.

The Lord Mayor's closing comments on the item were perhaps more revealing than he intended when he told the complaining residents in the public gallery to leave the Council Chamber, dismissing us with the words, 'This isn't your meeting. If you're not happy you can write in.'

If a meeting of all ward councillors doesn't belong to the constituents of those wards – including the residents in the public gallery – I'm not clear whose interests councillors think they serve when they sit in Chambers

But given their behaviour, perhaps neither are they.

## Things You Hear Around Portsmouth

### James Bicheno (2015)

If you are a visitor to this lovely island city of ours, you might overhear words and phrases you find curious, baffling or simply odd. While some of these might sound familiar, there may be some you don't know so well.

'Geez': short for 'Geezer', used to describe an unknown man or a friend, e.g. 'alright, Geez?'

'Mush' (pronounced 'Moosh'), used to refer to a person, e.g. 'some mush'; or as an informal way of address, e.g. 'oi, mush!'

'Bluarmy': name given to supporters of Portsmouth Football Club, reflecting the club's royal blue colours. Also pronounced 'blue-ar-my' or 'blarmy'.

'Dinlo': (also 'Din'), term of abuse, denoting an idiot or moron, e.g. 'He's well a din.'

'Squinny': (also 'Squin'), someone who is easily upset or hysterical.

'Pompey': 1) Gnaeus Pompeius the Great, 106 BC – 48 BC, Roman statesman and general. 2) Portsmouth.

'Got any fags?': 'Would you be so kind as to loan me a cigarette?'

'Got a light?': (pronounced 'Gotta loight?'), 'May I, perchance, trouble you to light said cigarette?'

'You startin'?': 'Are you seeking to disrupt the general good humour of the day?'

'D'ya wanna foight?': 'I challenge you to settle this dispute through combat.'

'Goin' dane tane': 'I am embarking on a journey to one of this island's commercial districts.'

'Give Stick/Take the Mick': make fun of, ridicule.

'Weeee!': conversational exclamation, 'By Jove!'

'Oi-oi!': 'Good day to you!'

'Chavved/Thieved/Taxed it': 'An act of larceny has been committed.'

'See look?'/'Know what I mean?': 'Do you comprehend?'

'Cushty': 'Splendid.'

'Sod ya': 'In light of your refusal to take up my offer I shall cease to consider you in future.'

'You're getting me at it!': 'You are trying my patience.'
'Well': 'Very', e.g. 'he was well a din', 'He was a complete idiot.
'Ease up': 'Do calm yourself.'
'Pack it up': 'Desist with your irritating behaviour.'
'Chuffed.': delighted.
'Reay!': 'Hoorah!'
'Matelot': personnel of a seagoing vessel.

## What's Going On? Addressing Commercial Media in Portsmouth

### Sophia Wood (2018)

I spend a lot of my day job talking to students about journalism and why it's important to local communities, to society and to democracy. I've done quite a lot of seminars and lectures looking at topics such as: what is the purpose of journalism, what do we want from our journalists, what role do journalists play in society, how does this relate to democracy and, increasingly, does it matter who owns the press.

In my view, the independent, non-advertising-funded model of media ownership is the ideal, even though most people today access their information from mainstream media provision, which is invariably commercially owned. My students also tend to agree that good journalism should provide us with the information we need to be citizens and to make informed decisions about our lives. Good journalism is about scrutinising the powerful and should provide a voice for everybody in – and for all sectors of – society.

I'm currently doing research into the representation of the Grenfell Tower fire and I'm interested in activities that help to involve people from the local community who have been affected by issues around flammable casing in their housing. In the same way, sites like S&C invite people into a conversation, including marginalised people who are usually only the subject of a discourse.

The revelation of injustice is another news value. Many of us here tonight will be familiar with the idea of the 'fourth estate'. Historically, this has been the idea of an independent press that provides checks against power whether it's located in the monarchy, the government or the clergy. Nowadays, we could add to that list the threat of advertising and commercially owned media. Many of us here will lament the degree to which commercialisation has undermined the fourth estate function of the media. Even before Trump and recent news agendas around fake news, we were living with a growing sense that the news media had become a business and not one that's run in the interests of society or the public good.

Media theorist Daniel Berkowitz wrote, 'Despite journalism's stated goal of depicting reality, the news media – tightly interlocked at top levels with powerful institutions – have an interest in preserving the larger, liberal capitalist system by helping maintain the boundaries of acceptable political discourse.' Berkowitz continues: 'The media establish what's normal and what's deviant by the way they portray people and ideas.' In my own teaching and research at the University of Portsmouth, I've looked at 'poverty porn', the demonisation of people on benefits and the representation of the European migrant crisis, which I think should be called the refugee crisis. I'm interested in how journalists within commercial enterprises often collude with the powerful.

Last week, the government announced very quietly the decision not to extend the work of the Leveson Inquiry into press standards. There will be no Leveson II, which was set to examine the relationship between the media and the police. The announcement was made while our largely deregulated national press were fixating on Snowmageddon. This was literally an example of 'a good day to bury bad news'.

Let's think about this in relation to Andrew Belsey's argument that 'the proper practice of journalism must sometimes be subversive and anti-establishment, and expose what those in power would rather keep concealed from the public to whom they should be accountable.' That's what good journalism is supposed to be. In reality, as we know from investigations like Leveson, we tend to find instead pacts between powerful elites, politicians who are supposed to represent us and global billionaire newspaper owners. The politicians court favourable coverage from the major papers in return for further deregulation of the media. I'm of a certain age now where I like to tyrannise my young students with references to Margaret Thatcher and her favour exchanges with Rupert Murdoch that paved the way to the deregulated media landscape we 'enjoy' today.

The result of all this, I think, has been a deepening public mistrust in mainstream journalists. They are now regarded as being down there with employees of the BBC in the 1970s. There's also a perception that journalism is dominated by mainly white, middle-class men. We've seen this recently in debates about the pay gap at the BBC. In January 2018, Carrie Gracie, the BBC's China editor, stepped down because she found out she was being paid less than her male counterparts. Then John Humphrys and John Sopel were caught on mike having a good old laugh at Gracie's failure to have attained the same pay scale as them. They also offered, in a joking way, to divert some of their inflated salaries towards her. These are the kinds of journalists who are out of touch with their audiences and the social challenges facing them: the housing crisis, uncertain employment in the 'gig economy', a feeling of powerlessness and dislocation, and a sense of being left behind by politics and the media.

To focus on the local context, David Harte has argued that 'the last decade has seen increasing agreement amongst scholars that local news has become less plural; less local in its orientation; less embedded in, and less reflective of, local communities; as well as less critical and independent from its (overwhelmingly elite) sources.'

If we're thinking about elite, non-inclusive or socially conservative views locally, I want to look at an opinion feature from 12th February 2018 in *The News*, our local print newspaper, by Clive Smith, who was making evident in this piece his aspiration to become the poor man's Katie Hopkins. 'Streets should be cleared of homeless for royal wedding,' he writes, adding his voice to the recent media non-story of Windsor Tory councillor Simon Dudley, who willingly became tabloid fodder with his suggestion that the homeless should be purged from that town lest the sight of their poverty ruin the royal wedding.

Smith goes on to state, 'Is it not like cleaning your house when you've got visitors coming? Look at Portsmouth, if you walk through town you can't miss the piles of sleeping bags, duvets and people lying in doorways. There is no way this looks good, it looks bad!' He goes on to compare the homeless to the 'Calais Jungle.'

I've spent twenty years studying the Holocaust and the demonisation of Jews in Nazi Germany, and I'm disturbed by this kind of demonisation of the poor and the powerless in the mainstream media today by people like Smith.

So how can local independent journalism salve the wounds made by local commercial journalism? It can offer us a sense of society, of democracy, of inclusion. As news provision moves online and audiences are able to interact with it, it's easier for public voices to be heard on these platforms.

As we've seen with S&C, investigative journalism is another key aspect here. Local officials and politicians must be held to account and readers should be able to contribute to the debate in a communal process of enlightenment rather than one of demonisation and trivia, which has come to dominate the political sphere.

As Christopher Ali argues, 'Local news is the lynchpin connecting community life to larger ideas like democracy in the public sphere. It's essential to community solidarity, identity and everyday life.'

## Mad Cows' Disease is Still a Threat to All of Us

### Christine Lord (2015)

**S&C: How did you come to write your book Who Killed My Son?**

I've worked as a journalist since I was sixteen. During the eighties, when BSE started killing cattle across the UK, I realised from my work in the media that information about the disease was being suppressed.

I was a single mum with a young son, Andrew, when the crisis started and I became so concerned that, from 1988, I banned all beef products from our diet. I had a daughter in 1990 and she's never eaten beef products. I wanted to keep my family safe and even then, I didn't believe what the media and the government were saying.

Andrew became ill in 2005. He became depressed and suffered from mood swings. I put it down to his age at first. He was a young man building a career in the media and suddenly he became quite introverted. He began losing work. Our GP diagnosed Andrew with anxiety. He had a series of tests and things seemed to settle down, for a while. But by early 2006, he suddenly became very thin. He was working even less. He wasn't the Andrew I knew at all. Our GP sent him to a counsellor and gave him anti-depressants, but Andrew told me, 'I'm not depressed, Mum, I just want to know what's wrong with me.'

By Christmas 2006, Andrew was becoming more and more reclusive, spending most of his time in his room. He was a totally different person. Before the illness, he was outgoing, social and very confident. He'd worked on a pilot for Sky television, and had been very close to becoming a presenter on CITV. He was always out with his friends.

The doctors kept running tests.

One day there was something on the TV about BSE. Andrew turned to me and said, 'I haven't got that, have I, Mum?'

'Of course not,' I told him.

But that night I lay awake and mentally ran through all Andrew's symptoms. I died a little bit that night as I realised my son probably had Variant CJD, the human form of Mad Cows Disease.

The next time we went to the hospital, I spoke to the doctors about my fear. They dismissed it at first. But after more tests, the doctors discovered he was dying from vCJD. I know now that Andrew's experience of diagnosis is common. GPs are not aware of the symptoms. Like many members of the public, they think it is a disease that has gone away.

Unfortunately, it isn't. Variant CJD (vCJD) continues to kill.

One in 2000 of us are either carrying or incubating the disease, which has incubation periods of up to 50 years. There is an ongoing risk for generations of people.

*Who Killed My Son?* is about my family's journey through illness, bereavement and loss. It uncovers the political and ongoing implications of BSE for the public, now and for future generations, and the lies the public were told about the disease.

The book is part of a campaign – Justice 4 Andy – to get justice for my son and for the thousands of people that are affected by this disease. It's part of a broader fight for safer food and safer health policies, including on blood and organ donation. The campaign also calls for full accountability for the victims of vCJD.

**What have you discovered about BSE and vCJD as a result of Andrew's death?**

In the book I say that what I've found out is like a dystopian sci-fi novel.

I uncovered that as early as 1985 – 86, the government knew that if someone ate infected BSE material, it could kill them. The basic facts were covered up to protect the meat industries and the pharmaceutical industries – it was about money.

My son was killed at the altar of greed and money.

As a result of that cover-up, anyone in the UK who was alive in the eighties has been exposed to BSE. Infected material was in HRT, toothpaste, vaccines, baby food, school dinners, even vegetarian dishes because the food labelling was so bad. Blood is not screened for vCJD and medical instruments are not cleaned to eradicate the potential for contamination by the disease.

It's vital to raise awareness that vCJD is an ongoing risk. I'm a great supporter of blood donation and organ donation, but we need to make sure we're screening for vCJD because we're currently continuing to contaminate those supplies. We can screen donors, it's a simple test to screen for vCJD but the government are holding back because they don't want the public to know how many people are carrying it.

**Do you think people are aware that vCJD is still a risk?**

No. I'm still meeting families who have children in their twenties who are dying from vCJD now, but most people think the risk is in the past.

The Department of Health is aware of 'silent carriers' of the disease, which means they remain well but they have been implicated in passing blood to people who have then died from vCJD. There's one donor I know of who gave blood for twenty years and is now linked to three deaths from BSE.

A lot of people don't realise that anyone who lived or worked in the UK for more than 3 months between 1980 and 1996 cannot give blood in the USA and other countries because internationally, it's recognised that we are all at risk of vCJD. I choose not to give blood because I could be at risk. My campaign fights for all blood donors to be screened. The risk has not gone away.

**Who Killed My Son? is a tragic and devastating story. How did you approach the writing of the book?**

When Andrew became ill, he told me, 'Mum, whatever's wrong with me, find out who did this to me, sue them and make sure this never happens to anyone else.'

His request has become my mission.

I've always kept written and photographic diaries. When Andrew became ill, I also began to keep a video diary. I wanted to have a record, not just as a mother, but in terms of factually documenting what was happening to us. All that material went into the book and the campaign.

I also undertook a lot of research about BSE and Variant CJD. I have a vast library of documents and reports that I cite in the book, which are also available on the campaign website. I interviewed – or in some cases, tried to interview – government ministers who had been involved in the crisis. All that material became the foundation of the book. After the initial shock of Andrew dying, I worked with a friend on it and it took about eight months to write.

When I was writing the book, one of the problems was that I had too much material to include. So, I'm preparing a second book called *What Killed My Son?* The first book took us up to 2011, and the second will bring us up to now.

I've also made three documentaries, which you can access on the website.

**The book uncovers a long-term government campaign to mislead the public. Do you think this scandal has any implications for our understanding of democracy in the UK?**

Absolutely. What the public must realise is that every powerful minister and MP in Westminster have their own press crews, sometimes of up to 30-40 people, whose job it is to manipulate stories, to shape them, or to stop stories going out altogether.

I'm very interested in the Independent Inquiry into Child Sexual Abuse as the first round of allegations and news stories about that scandal occurred at the same time as the BSE crisis. In 2015, I wrote to Simon Danczuk offering to share my experiences because I believe there is a crossover between that inquiry and my investigation into BSE. Ministers at the time were covering up BSE and that would have left them very open to manipulation and the possibility of corruption.

I believe we need some form of radical change within government. Even prior to Andrew being ill, I'd interviewed many MPs – on and off the record – and it's obvious that our political system is still an old boys' network. If you're powerful enough within government, it's possible to be above the law and no one should be above the law, no matter who you are. Government regulates itself. They set their own salaries and when something goes wrong, they investigate themselves. Frankly, it stinks!

My hope centres on the young MPs I've interviewed who are starting to come into our political system, from all parties. They are idealistic, full of hope, they want change. Unfortunately, the further you go up the greasy pole in politics, the more corrupt you have to become to keep that position. I'd like to see the country get rid of that old blood in politics because they are manipulating the press, freedom of speech and fundamentally, our democracy.

**How has the government's failure to acknowledge the truth vCJD impacted on the families affected by the disease?**

It's absolutely devastating. I'm a qualified counsellor as well as a qualified journalist, so I have quite a lot of insight into bereavement, both personally and professionally.

One of the most devastating things when you lose a child, particularly if they were killed unlawfully (and my barristers have told me that Andrew was definitely killed unlawfully) and there is no trial, no punishment, no accountability for their death, it just adds to the trauma suffered by the family.

John Gummer, Margaret Thatcher, John Major and others should be held responsible in a court of law for the deaths that their lies caused. But no one has been found accountable for those deaths, and they're still happening.

Families of victims are routinely intimidated not to speak out. Lots of the families who spoke to me asked to remain anonymous for that reason. For the families of victims, we know our children must have been infected by the food or medicines we gave our children. When your child is infected, families are told not to tell people about it, they're made to feel as if it's something shameful. I've met families who have been told explicitly by health professionals that their child is sick because the parents gave them 'cheap meat'. That guilt compounds the trauma. Many families affected by vCJD have suffered mental health issues, they're unable to work or lose their careers. They're utterly traumatised.

I'm traumatised by Andrew's death, but I suppose I've been able to channel my emotions outwards in a constructive manner. I still have black days even now because Andrew was my future and I miss him every single day. The way he died haunts me because vCJD is such a brutal disease.

**In the book you write about receiving anonymous threats to yourself and your family during the campaign. How did you deal with that?**

When you hold your 24-year-old, once fit and healthy, young son in your arms as he dies; when you've watched him become blind, deaf, quadriplegic, suffering from dementia; when you've watched that confident, successful child slowly lose everything he loved in life in such a slow, cruel way; when you've watched all that, you're not afraid anymore.

I'm not afraid anymore because the worst thing that could ever have happened, has happened. I think that makes me quite dangerous to the establishment. I'm not frightened of them. I'm not frightened of anything or anyone.

I was offered £120,000 by the government as a 'no fault, no blame' package. I told them to stick it. I'm not a wealthy woman, but I cannot be bought, I cannot be silenced and I cannot be corrupted.

**Have you ever worried about being sued?**

Never. I'd welcome it. Bring it on, John Gummer. Bring it on Kenneth Clarke, I'll see you in court.

I've never had as much as a solicitor's letter, even when the book was published.

Off camera, I've had threats from John Gummer, I've received threats over the phone. I've received subtle threats from various individuals unknown to me at public events. The intimidation is undercover, it wears a benign face. I think that's more dangerous. I call them creatures of the night. They'll come on *Question Time*, present themselves as good guys but underneath, they're very dangerous, sinister people.

**Where does the campaign go from here?**

Since the Conservatives have been back in government it's been quite hard to move forward with the campaign because of the relationships between past and present ministers. Despite this, I'm very upbeat. Things are moving forward slowly.

In 2014, there was a government inquiry into blood safety and the risk of vCJD and I gave written and oral evidence to the inquiry panel (After the storm? UK blood safety and the risk of variant Creutzfeldt-Jakob Disease). The Science and Technology Committee concluded that we need to screen blood donors for vCJD and recommended the government: to undertake a study to find out the prevalence of vCJD, to screen for those at risk of it, and to explore whether incidents of vCJD in the elderly are being misdiagnosed as dementia.

The government published the final inquiry report on a Friday night and the media barely picked it up. David Cameron has ignored the recommendations put forward by the panel.

But I remain hopeful.

When we launched the campaign website, we had a million hits in one day. People from all over the world contact me every day to share stories of their loved ones who are dying or have died from vCJD.

Whether the government likes it or not, this is a story that isn't going to go away.

## Re-thinking Britain, Re-thinking Portsmouth

### Dianna Djokey (2015)

I am a firm believer in the power of museums to challenge people's way of thinking. In 2015, I was invited to visit the Greenwich Maritime Museum's *Re-think* exhibition (now ended) exploring the human story of immigration to Britain, which challenges some of the more negative narratives surrounding migration and refugees. I was reminded of Portsmouth's own struggles with the issue of refugees and I began to reflect on the role the city's museums can play in challenging negative local perceptions towards migrants and refugees who make their home in Portsmouth.

The Re-think exhibition was developed in partnership with the Migration Museum and the International Maritime Organisation (IMO) and emphasised the human stories of migrants and refugees. For me, the timing of the exhibition couldn't have been better. As the refugee crisis in Europe played across our screens, the exhibition pulled visitors out of the media storm, reminding us that each statistic and soundbite hides a human being.

Most powerfully, the exhibition asked questions like: *what does home mean to you? or what would you take with you if you were moving to another country?* But the question that resonated with me the most was *how much do you feel that Britain's migration story is your story too?*

The last question is the one I would like to ask the majority of museums in Portsmouth.

In October 2015, Portsmouth City Council voted in favour of asking the government that Portsmouth no longer be a hub for asylum seekers. The motion passed with 21 votes to 16 and was met with anger and disappointment by many protesting locals in the city.

With this vote in mind, I realised how much still needs to be done to change attitudes to migration and asylum locally. Much of this work takes place with and across the local community: for example, through inspiring projects like Don't Hate Donate. But our museums have a role to play too, both in reflecting the stories of, and reaching out to, local communities.

How do local museums tell the story of migration in Portsmouth?

There has been some great work from the Portsmouth Museums Service as part of their Oral History Project to collect stories from local Bangladeshi, Chinese and Caribbean communities, for example, although this work is some years past now. However, many museums around Portsmouth tend to be conservative in their outreach work, keeping within what they know, and staying firmly inside their own comfort zone. The manager of Portsmouth Museums, Dr Jane Mee, highlighted this herself in a 2009 article in the Museums Journal titled: 'Why are we so cautious when we could be bold and challenging?'

Portsmouth's cultural heritage is impressive and ranked 9th nationally for local heritage and related activities in 2015 in the national Heritage Index. But the future of culture and tourism should not rely on the well-used – and well known – history of the city. We need to build inclusion within our communities and within the arts and heritage sector so that our understanding of Portsmouth's heritage grows ever more rich and diverse, and as a key way of increasing the city's social capital.

Museums can be the bridge stretching local communities towards this goal.

Greenwich Maritime Museum's *Re-Think* exhibition shows the many ways museums can engage local communities in a meaningful way and I would like to see Portsmouth building on the success of past projects like the *Voices of Portsmouth* oral history project. But too often such projects are a one-off, they are not embedded in how we reflect and tell the stories of our communities, wherever in the world they originated. Too often, our migrant communities and refugee groups become 'stakeholders' who are called upon to give views, feedback or contributions to existing projects run by heritage and cultural organisations, but rarely embedded at the heart of the museum itself.

The way we tell the stories of our city needs to change. We can't treat the inclusion of marginalised communities like throwing a dog a bone once in a blue moon to keep them happy. Instead, we must work hard in our museums and broader cultural institutions to include all our communities in the everyday running of museums, as well as in the design and delivery of the exhibitions on display there. This should be our benchmark and our norm – after all, policy conversations about diversity and inclusion in heritage and culture have been going on for more than 20 years, at least. How much more discussion is needed for the sector to demonstrate that museums are not only about the artefacts they exhibit, but about people?

As organisations located in local communities it is our responsibility to let our most marginalised residents know museums are listening. When the Council closes doors with the voice of hostility, our culture and heritage organisations can extend a welcome to refugees and migrants in Portsmouth that shows we stand with them, as part of the city's story.

My advice to Portsmouth museums? Talk to communities. Work with them. We have the tools to do it. This may mean your work may get harder, more challenging, but if as an organisation you care about diversity and inclusiveness within your audiences, the rewards will be huge.

Our changing communities are our future heritage, just as they were in our past. The babies of refugees hoping to begin a new life in Portsmouth are the future leaders of our cultural and heritage sectors.

*'To tell you de truth I don't really know where I belaang. Yes, divide de ocean, divide to de bone. Wherever I hang me knickers – that's my home.'* Grace Nichols, poet, 1989. (Quote used in the Re-think exhibition)

## See-Throughs

## Mark R. Wright (2018)

He peers into the mannequin's transparent head and raps lightly against the side. *Knock knock knock.* 'Nothing in here.'

She doesn't laugh, and she didn't laugh the other times he did it. Today, she hasn't laughed much at all. The most he has got from her is a smile and an accompanying breath through her nose, like the residual gas of a laugh that is no longer there. She is stiff and tense, a world apart from the coffees, the dinners, the walks along the road to Blackheath Common. She is flattened, and he thinks – he worries – that she is not enjoying herself.

He stops in front of the last mannequin. He looks into its head at the open vase of its neck, but he doesn't repeat the joke.

She's probably got it by now.

He wants a reaction from her. From his clowning. She pretends to smile. Or does she? Can you pretend to smile?

Another woman is in the room with them. The other woman is slim and well-dressed, with a broad-brim hat and a chiffon scarf on her shoulders. She is carrying a brochure and a small bag and seems to take an interest in the installation, seems to be there for the art. But the other woman has also smirked at the 'joke'. Nothing in here. The same line, three times over. And three smirks. What does that woman see that she isn't seeing? What is the punch-line? They can all see there is nothing in there.

She watches the woman with the scarf try to catch his eye, but he doesn't notice. He is busy with the mannequins. The woman looks around the installation, pinches her brochure between elbow and hip and moves to the next section.

And now it is just the two of them.

A seated mannequin is facing her. It has a pair of headphones clamped either side of its clear head.

She leans a little closer to see if there's music playing.

He puts his arm around one of the mannequins' shoulders and strikes an identical pose. Arm in the air as if reading the same book, head angled down as if thinking the same thoughts.

She doesn't look.

He holds the stance long enough to feel foolish. Eventually, he relaxes and moves on. On one wall of the sheer-white room hangs a large painting. The background is fiery, orange-burning-to-yellow. A wavy green chord snakes through the foreground, hanging between open scissor blades.

A standing mannequin stares blankly up at it.

'This one looks cheery,' he says. *'Alien Medical School'.*

Her face is still down by the headphones; she answers with her back to him. 'It's not about the painting,' she says.

He hasn't been to a lot of art galleries, but he's always thought paintings were quintessentially art. Has he misunderstood art, or has he misunderstood the word 'quintessentially'? He looks around the room, trying to work out what it is about. He is more of a fan of what he calls 'honest paintings': men in suits and women in lampshade-dresses punting on the river with tea and sticky buns. Starry nights, dogs playing poker. It is what it is. No need for forensic dissection, no *CSI Warhol.*

No need for people to feel left out.

Before her he went on few dates, met with few women. He is in his early thirties but looks at the rest of his thirties, and his forties, and his life like a schoolboy looks at the last ten minutes of an exam. He is urgent to be with someone, urgent to be safe. He wants for her to laugh, for her to like him, but large dolls, paintings-that-aren't-paintings – what's it supposed to mean?

He tilts his head at the canvas and tries to make sense of it.

She watches him: head askew, studying the art. It has always amused her, this idea that turning your perspective those ninety degrees will solve the mystery, that paintings aren't hung the right way for a reason. Is that too critical? Maybe. She just wants this to go well.

This is their fifth date, and she's wondering how it will end. She is in her mid-thirties now. She has met a lot of men that say what they think she wants to hear to have sex with her, and then that is that. It doesn't matter if they agree with it, or believe it, or whether it was their own thought or not. She had been a warm body for a dark night and damn the outcome.

She isn't prudish but, for her, sex is the start of something and she doesn't want to start something that isn't right. No time wasting. Not anymore.

The installation's centre display is an open book on a lectern so thin a library cough could snap it. A mannequin stands with its back to her, its clear eyes directed at the text. She hovers behind it, chin on its shoulder, hands on its hips for balance.

She picks a place and begins to read:

*He sighs. The young in one another's arms, heedless, engrossed in the sensual music. No country, this, for old men. He seems to be spending a lot of time sighing. Regret: a regrettable note on which to go out.*

She's suddenly aware of the intimacy of her position, and her hands feel improper on the figure. She lets go. 'This quote is beautiful. Do you think it's part of the theme?' Caught in the spotlights, he doesn't move. He just purses his lips and shrugs. She sighs. They look away from each other and pretend to study at the art.

There was a small exhibition in Kent – 'Vacuum' – a field trip from university some fifteen years before. She and her lecturer had stood, side by side, by a box containing a small wooden figure, some bits of leaf, some old twig. She had felt the warmth of his fingers as they brushed against hers, and felt the thrill of his voice, his attention, his thoughts. *A lot of people do emptiness by leaving the box empty. Notice how bare this looks for the smaller objects inside? Spaced out, individual.* He breathed against her. *Apart.*

Those unethical months with him were a wonder, a snow globe between student- and work-life. Saturdays were for art and trendy bars, Sundays for wine and deep conversation in bed. *How does this affect you? How would you do it? Why do you think it works?* Attention on her, interest in her thoughts. Days happened, and time was little more than a sound a clock made from a wall in another room.

Of course, it didn't last. It was sure and crucial, and then it was sharp and painful. No galleries, no discussions. Her clothes in bags on the pavement; someone else upstairs. Everything and then nothing. After him, she'd been with boys who didn't care to open that part of her, and her thoughts all withered on the vine. She had tried not to compare, but a first love sticks and the years make them a giant. She was spaced out, individual. Apart.

This is her first museum visit for a while. She can feel the awareness returning – she loves how the mannequins are set, their simulation of looking. *Just say one thing, have one thought. Please.*

Her eyes are drawn to the tendril painting.

Alien Medical School. That thought is stuck in her head.

There are different types of looking: appreciative, analytical. Observational. That last one is dirty: the least impressive, least likely to wow her, and most apposite to describe him. On the left side of the room is the tendril painting; beside that is a book on a stand; and, beside that, a large music deck on a table with chunky, wired headphones. The headphones cover the ears of a transparent mannequin seated in a wooden chair.

Gazing towards the exit.

In front of both the painting and the book are two more see-through figures, staring at the works. None of the three are wearing clothes. Their heads are bald, their features neutral. He can't say what they mean, but he's noticed the dummies have heads, where the ones in Primark finish at the neck.

No one is going to care about that.

'What do you think?' she asks suddenly.

'It's very interesting.'

'What do you think it means?'

He screws up his face as though he's thinking. 'That art is superficial.'

'How so?'

He shrugs. The lights are hot and there's sweat on his face. 'I don't know. I'm not very good at this.'

'It's just looking.'

Just a *type* of looking. He tries harder. 'Is it saying that art is immortal? That it will live on, survive, in some way.' He scoots down, scuttles to the other side of the mannequin beside her, and rises with the figure standing between them. 'Appreciated by goldfish-bowl men of the future.'

Her face, warped by the contours of the clear head, gazes blankly back.

'Or appreciated by no one. Just...existing.' He takes his head away from the mannequin's and sees he has left a misty patch of sweat on its forehead. He licks his thumb and hastily wipes it away. 'You know there's probably someone who works here who we can ask-'

'No.'

'-dying of boredom-'

'No.' Firmer this time. 'I don't want to ask.'

'Why not?'

'I want us to work it out.'

'Asking would save time.'

'It's not about the time.'

Not about art; not about time. What is it about? What is it about? 'Give me a clue.'

'The answer is just what you think.'

'That mannequins can't read.'

'No.'

'That art is blind.'

'Why?'

'I don't *know*.' He flaps his arms against his sides. 'Why does everything have to be interpreted? What's the bloody point?'

'It's important.'

'Bollocks. What else that matters is drawn out like this? Would your doctor pin your stomach x-ray on the cabinet and be like, *Your diagnosis will have to wait, Ms Walsh; I'll need to interpret whether that dark patch is a bagel or a tumour.*'

'Now you're just being stupid.'

And that ends it. She stares fixedly at the seated mannequin, and he wanders to the other side of the space and stands there and doesn't say anything because this is the closest he has come to crying from something someone has said since he was at school.

She peers through a doorway; it's a projector room. Images jump on the walls.

She doesn't want any more. This trip has stirred her up, and now the 'stupid' comment is hanging between them. He's standing in the corner, and she's ready to give up when out of nowhere – out of less than nowhere – he says: 'Is it saying that art is meaningless?'

She stops. For a moment, all five figures are still. 'Why do you say that?'

'I think maybe the mannequins don't understand.' He looks down, shuffles between his feet. 'Art is just bits of things, really. A surface, some paint. A message you don't always get. Maybe they're see-through because they're empty, because they don't get it. Maybe, without the right person to appreciate it, it doesn't really mean anything at all.'

She stares at him. Her heart skips, and she can't help but grin. She is so taken aback that all she can say is: 'That's brilliant.'

He gives her an awkward smile. 'Got there in the end.'

Suddenly she sees herself: stern, introverted. What does this mean, what does that mean. 'I'm sorry,' she says. She takes hold of his hand. 'I just wanted to know.' He's looking ahead to the projector room but she shakes her head. 'How about we get some food?' She then adds meaningfully: 'Maybe at mine.'

She knows her demeanour has switched, and wonders for one terrifying second if, after all that, he'll guilt her, or just flat out refuse. He thinks for a bit – or pretends to think, if you can do that – before he brightens and affects a comic wince. 'No interpreting?'

She squeezes his hand. 'Promise.'

He scoops his arm around her shoulders and leads her back towards her room, towards the start of something.

Shielded on the other side of his body, growing smaller and smaller as they leave, is a thick plastic tablet. Inside is a piece of paper with some lines of printed text.

(Italicised quote borrowed from *Disgrace* by J.M. Coetzee, p.190.)

**From the Artist:** *'The See-Throughs' by Jennifer Shaw 'came from the sudden thought that art is just bits of things: a surface, some paint; and a message you don't always get...'*

## A Map of the Solent

### Tom Phillips (2015)

You can't beat a good map. That's what I say. Right now, on the wall opposite me are a map of the world – which I'd like to think isn't a sign of incipient megalomania – and an illustrated street plan of Sofia in Bulgaria – which has its own story. Over the years, their predecessors have included a rail map of Europe (from Inter-railing days); a road map of America's Eastern Seaboard (from an adolescent trip to South Carolina); and a map of the air corridors across what was then the Soviet Union which my father, a flight engineer with British Airways, 'retrieved' from the flight deck of a Boeing 707 after flying from Moscow to Tokyo shadowed by Mig fighters. Oddly, the first map I remember sticking up on my bedroom wall when I was ten or eleven was an Ordnance Survey inch-to-the-mile map of Portsmouth, the Isle of Wight and the Solent.

I only say 'oddly' because I didn't live anywhere near the south coast. I grew up in Buckinghamshire, very close to one of those places which claim to be the furthest point from the sea in Britain. Our own village's claim to fame was that it had been the scene of the Great Train Robbery in 1963 – the year my father bought our house, although the timing is presumably coincidental. Rather than sticking up a map of Buckinghamshire, however (with Bridego Bridge, Leatherslade Farm and other sites made famous by Reynolds, Biggs & co circled in pencil), my pre-teen self went for the old red-covered version of what's now known as OS Landranger 196.

This wasn't due to landlocked yearning for the sea or a longstanding family connection with that part of the country. It was simply because I'd been on a primary school trip to Portsmouth and the Isle of Wight and, having already spotted the symptoms of my nascent cartophilia, my father had bought me a copy of the map as a present – even though, on reflection, it would've been better if he'd given it to the teacher who managed to get us lost on a walk to Alum Bay.

That map stayed on the wall beside my bed for three years before it was replaced by photos of Joe Strummer and Debbie Harry torn from the pages of NME. Like my train set and my Willard Price novels, it went into a box and then into the loft. I've still got it. It's in a filing cabinet with the American road map and the airline map of the Soviet Union.

I should have retrieved it and put it in my rucksack when we went on holiday this summer. For reasons known only to teenage boys, my son suddenly developed a passionate interest in submarines. Around the same time, my wife, who's been tracing our family history, discovered that one of my ancestors was Thomas 'Customer' Smythe, a Tudor-era chap with a spectacular ginger beard and head honcho of Customs and Excise at London docks. Given these circumstances, it was almost inevitable that our holiday would end up consisting of two days in Portsmouth, with most of our time spent nosing around the Historic Dockyard, the Mary Rose and HMS Alliance.

It's possible that my old map might have come in handy when we went to find our hotel. Or maybe not. I don't seem to remember there being quite so many dual carriageways on the map as there were on the ground. Either way, the initially confident journey turned into a psychogeographical ramble into Buckland which eventually brought us out, not at our hotel, but at Dickens' birthplace and a brief, unexpected moment of literary homage which I wouldn't have otherwise managed to infiltrate into our official sub- and Tudor warship-dominated itinerary. Adding to the pleasure of surprise was the fact that the house looks so ... well, Dickensian, to the point at which I half-expected the cast of Oliver! to come bounding out of the front door singing 'Consider Yourself' while Mr Brownlow looked on benevolently from an upstairs window. Three years previously the house had been the venue for the launch of an anthology to mark the Dickens centenary: one of my poems had been in the book. Not long afterwards, the anthology's editor – a friend of mine in Reading – started visiting the Isle of Wight on a fairly regular basis. There was a fairly decent chance, I thought, that while we were standing outside 393 Old Commercial Road he was heading towards Portsmouth to catch the ferry. Our paths may even have crossed at Portsmouth Harbour that same afternoon.

It's that kind of coincidence which seems to haunt every visit to Portsmouth. The following day, for example, we continued our excursions through the Historic Dockyard, picking up the kind of random facts – World War II submariners stank because they never washed, nineteenth-century sailors weren't any shorter than their modern-day equivalents – that usually stick in my mind far longer than all the official stuff about admirals, deployments and engagements. It being nearly the hundredth anniversary of Gallipoli, preparations were well underway for commemorative activities. The flags of the nations that had participated in the campaign had been put up; naval personnel were double-checking the arrangements; a group of actors was rehearsing on the deck of Gallipoli veteran HMS M.33. We were twenty-four hours too early and would be back in Bristol when the main event took place.

Which sounds as if it should count as an almost perfect lack of coincidence – except that, the following day, another friend of ours, one from Bristol, would almost certainly be standing exactly where we were, leaning on the rail, watching the actors on board HMS M.33. She was coming to the Gallipoli Centenary because she'd worked on the display about the campaign in the museum. Anna was also the friend who'd been part of a deci decidedly unlikely coincidence the previous year. I've written elsewhere about the chance meeting with a Bulgarian student in Portsmouth which had all manner of unexpected consequences, but there was another upshot of that brief encounter. When I was visiting Sofia and Vassi's family were planning my trip to the Black Sea coast, I posted on Facebook that I was in Bulgaria and about to catch a bus to the seaside. Almost immediately, Anna messaged to say that she was in Bulgaria too, taking part in a theatre project. In Sozopol. On the Black Sea coast. Vassi was scribbling my itinerary on the back of an envelope at the time: first stop, Sozopol.

The following day I got off the coach from Sofia. It's a popular resort, Sozopol, but with Bulgarians rather than Brits, so it's not turned into the peak-season hellhole that is Sunny Beach further up the coast. Anna was waiting outside the Bar Small Tequila, on the narrow strip of land that connects old Sozopol with new. Even though we both live in Bristol, I couldn't remember the last time we'd met. Maybe a year before. Now we were catching up, swapping news about kids and work and mutual friends over bottles of Burgasko in a bar beside the Black Sea. Statistically speaking, it seemed, there was more chance of us meeting on the other side of the continent than on the harbourside at home.

The theatre company Anna was working with were in town for the Apollonia festival, the Bulgarian seaside equivalent of Edinburgh Fringe. A joint Bulgarian-Romanian venture, the company specialised in 'labyrinth' theatre and were going to be in the town museum the next day. I told Anna I'd be there and then went back to what was becoming our favourite topic: the sheer unlikelihood of our meeting by chance in the seaside town of Sozopol.

In the morning, I got up early, wandered through old Sozopol under dark-beamed balconies and had a conversation with an old man in a sailor's cap about the relative strength of the off-sea breeze. Trawlers slumped against harbourside wharves. At the far end of the isthmus a row of concrete Xs formed the town's coastal defences. Languid holiday-makers stationed themselves outside cafes selling deep slices of cake while kids chased along cobbled alleys. Somewhere someone was rehearsing a Tennessee Williams play translated into Bulgarian. I met Anna and the theatre company for lunch before we walked to the museum. I thought it was just going to be a leisurely tourist visit. Half-an-hour later, I was perched on the back of a chair in an upstairs gallery, making up a monologue in the character of a 4,000-year-old Thracian cult object as part of an on-the-spot site-specific theatre piece. Fortunately, the human audience seemed to find this bit of unexpected improv somewhat more hilarious than the 4,000-year-old Thracian cult object in the cabinet behind me did – and the Margaritas in the old town jazz bar we retreated to certainly tasted all the better afterwards.

Does any of this have anything to do with that map of the Solent I used to have on my bedroom wall? I doubt it. I don't know. In a cafe on The Hard, we ate full English breakfasts and in the newspaper headlines some business leader or other was quoted about having a clear and well-defined roadmap. We went out into the street to smoke before catching the train back to Bristol. The flat-bottomed ferry to Ryde slunk past. If only the inventor of Blu-Tack had been from Portsmouth instead of Leicester.

## How Playing Dungeons and Dragons in Portsmouth Slayed My Anxiety

### Claire Pearse (2017)

Imagine you're in the depths of an enchanted forest; a large orc is fast approaching. What do you do? Fight? Flee? Negotiate? Imagine that the trees are now buildings in Portsmouth, and that the orc is a stranger approaching you in the street? Would you have the bravery to talk to them? Or would you run?

Thankfully there aren't any orcs in Portsmouth but, for some people, bumping into a fellow human being on the street can be as scary as encountering a fantastical monster. According to Birmingham University, 1 in 10 children suffer from a diagnosable mental illness, yet only 1 in 4 receive treatment for it. The same study estimates that, by 2020, 1 in 3 teenagers will have access to mental health treatment. With government cuts depriving young people of the care they need, is it time to consider more inventive or creative treatments?

Given that two of the main drivers of depression are loneliness and social fear, any therapy that builds confidence is welcome. For the last two years of studying at the University of Portsmouth, I've been spending my weekend nights playing *Dungeons and Dragons* (*D&D*) and have found this to be a much more rewarding experience than getting hammered at the Student Union. *D&D* is a table-top role-playing game with a straightforward premise: you only need a set of D20 (20-sided) dice, a miniature figure, a pencil and paper, and your imagination. A group of players take on the roles of characters with a range of alignments, backgrounds and classes. One player is nominated the Dungeon Master (DM), who devises the goals and parameters of the game.

Many well-known celebrities have played, including actor James Franco, author Stephen King and politician Michael Gove.

Night-clubbing or dice-rolling – which is most socially fulfilling? You can imagine the answer most young people would give. It's seen to be socially beneficial to 'put yourself out there' in a club, as a confidence-boosting move infinitely preferable to 'shutting yourself off' from the outside world and escaping into an imagined universe.

To test that theory, I reached out to the people it might apply to: the members of High Rollers, a *D&D* group run by the Bristol-based Yogscast YouTube channel on the streaming website Twitch. I asked them if playing *D&D* had helped improve their social skills.

Chris Trott, a YouTuber and former student at the University of Portsmouth, agreed it had. 'Without *D&D*,' he said, 'I wouldn't be gaming three times a week with different social groups.' Katie Morrison, an acting graduate and Talent Manager for Multiplay, told me that two things had greatly developed her confidence in college: acting and *D&D*. 'It gets you to see your friends,' she said. The Dungeon Master of the stream and Community Manager for Yogscast, Mark Hulmes, told me, '*D&D* improves your life skills, social skills and problem solving.'

Based in Providence, Rhode Island, Ethan Gilsdorf is a journalist and author of the awarding-winning book *Fantasy Freaks and Gaming Geeks – An Epic Quest for Reality Among Role Players, Online Gamers and Other Dwellers of Imaginary Realms*. In a TEDx talk, Gilsdorf discusses 5 different lessons that *D&D* teaches to help people in the real world: collaboration, innovation, character-building, tolerance and the power of imagination.

Gilsdorf's own experiences of *D&D* taught him teamwork and problem-solving, and that rushing into conflict isn't always the answer to the challenges that arise in both real life and in the game. 'There's no shame in a well bargained escape,' he argues. 'Don't fight. Negotiate.' He also believes that *D&D* gives its players an environment in which to take risks and fail in a safe way, which generates the kind of wisdom needed to take on real-life risks. There are also opportunities to develop compassion by interacting with different people and creatures. 'I can think about that bully I encountered with a little more empathy,' Gilsdorf says.

Finally, he asserts that, in the digital age, we have become passive consumers of packaged narratives: players of computer games like Call of Duty or Super Mario must follow fairly strict plot arcs, their actions restricted by a handful of locations, objects and characters. With *D&D*, however, a player's imagination is the only limitation. 'The key to confidence and the key to self-reliance is in controlling your own narrative, telling your own story.' Gilsdorf says. 'And stories connect us, stories provide hope. Deep inside all of us, inside our metaphorical dungeons, there is a dragon, but we don't know if we can slay it or befriend it unless we try.'

I can vouch for Gilsdorf and say that *D&D* has made me more resilient and helped me overcome the metaphorical dragon of my anxiety. Not only did it help me, it helped *D&D* players from all over the world.

Charley Micu, a third year student at the University of Portsmouth, told me, 'DMing [playing the Dungeon Master], in particular, really helped me feel comfortable being myself. In other settings I would feel out of place, but the game built my confidence a lot.' Katrine Dankertsen from Egersund, Norway, said, '*D&D* helped me to find other people with the same interests as me, and thanks to that I have made a lot of new friends.' Sam Elgart, a middle school student from Virginia, says the game helped her to become more outgoing. 'Creating my own stories, and building new universes and characters has improved my confidence, and gotten me to enjoy my creative side a lot more.'

That the very first edition of *D&D*, released in 1974, had a male-dominated audience makes it even more exciting that the above players I spoke to were all female. Not only does it counter the stereotype of *D&D* as a game only for introverted, anti-social boys, it shows that it's an inclusive game for all genders and all ages – indeed anyone who wants to become more worldly and self-reliant.

I know it's a stretch to suggest that *D&D* can single-handedly solve the epidemic of depression amongst young people suffering, but I feel that collaborative, creative and social gaming can be a step in the right direction. Dr Raffael Boccamazzo, the Clinical Director of Take This, a non-profit charitable organisation that promotes awareness of mental illness, told me that he uses *D&D* to assist teenagers who have difficulties with socialising. 'Kids who were previously unable even to maintain eye contact started to take commanding roles in the games they played,' he said.

Let's hope that other therapists follow Dr Boccamazzo's lead and we can slay a few more demons of depression. So, in the words of Ethan Gilsdorf: 'Arm yourself with pencil and graph paper, gather around the fire of each other's imaginations and go on an adventure.'

**Owl & Pussy-Cat #Revisited (Slight Return/Visa Denied)**
**William Sutton, with apologies to Edward Lear (2018)**

The Owl and the Pussy-cat went to sea
    In a government subsidised ferry
With dreams of Quorn mince served with M&S quince,
    And prosecco to make the guests merry.
The Owl filled out Puss's visa form,
    And sang to an old sitar,
'O lovely Pussy! O Pussy, my love,
What an exotic Pussy you are,
        You are,
        You are!
What a well-travelled Pussy you are!'

They cross-questioned the Owl, leaving Puss there to scowl.
    'So. How long does this 'spouse' plan to visit?'
'But if we are marrying, what limit to tarrying?'
    'This collar – engagement ring, is it?'
They detained them all day, separate cells, no parlay,
    Checked their bags and identifications,
Summoning down to the centre that well-known dementor,
The Home Office Rep for Immigration,
        migration,
        privation,
Devotee of repatriation.

'What you got in them paws? Are you travelling with claws?'
    'Must you really so frantically frisk us?'
'E'er suffered a seizure? Let's see this spouse visa.
    Seek asylum?' Growled Puss, 'Off my whiskers.'
'To prove love genuine, provide pics, Valentine's,
    Love poems – and bank account flush, mate.'
So they stamped her REMOVE, pending Owl's chance to prove:

*Available maintenance funds equivalent to a minimum gross annual
income of £18,600 per annum, each time the migrant applies for
temporary leave to remain as a family member,*
    *and once eligible for Indefinite Leave to Remain (usually after five
years), Government requirements supporting integration & preventing
burdens on taxpayers.*

So the Owl is no slob, and he slaves at his job.
    Gets his Government Gateway Tax Number
Fills the forms in online, till it beeps Out of Time.
    His USER password? – Can't remember.
Keep on planning their marriage. Th'Home Office miscarriage
    Of justice just bureaucrat's muddle.
If he keeps slaving hard, he'll earn her that green card
    And she'll one day escape Calais' jungle
        They'll struggle,
        Or else smuggle,
Her in through that dark Eurotunnel.

So those Kwiki-Mart aisles Owl stacks up with sad smiles,
    Shifting gherkins, jerk chickens, & turkey.
Fears employer harassment, has no health assessment
    On this zero hours contract he's working.
Before his paychecks, tumbling fun bags of snacks
    Send him to Accident & Emergency.
He texts Puss in frustration: 'Need wing operation:
    But there's three months wait for non-emergency,
Though it hurts, you see,
        Jeremy Hunt, he
        Says, *"No crisis in NHS,"* you see.'

Puss replies, 'Don't be silly, Owl, claim Disability.
    Government will pay your rental.
The DWP don't accept his sick note
    And the forms they are driving him mental.
With Owl's broken wing, can't play sitar nor sing,
    Then his rent doubles with Bedroom Tax.
Soon he's out on the street, no bed, nothing to eat,
    Sleeping rough 'mid delinquents on smack
    From tic-tacs
    And Kit-Kats
    And Nik-Naks;
All so far from his wedding day tasks.'

So he goes helter-skelter twixt rough sleep and shelter,
    Subsists on food bank and soup kitchen.
With no home address, his sick claim's in a mess.
    And this country they dreamed they'd be rich in!
Owl's collapsed to his knees, by a pub where TVs
    Blare a broadcast of power strong and stable.
Never cursing his foul treatment, finally Owl
    Is defibrillated on the pavement
    So brave.
    Can they save him?
    Oh yeah!
But he dies on the operating table.

Still dreaming of marriage, Puss hallucinates a carriage
    To escape the Calais Jungle
Disdaining all laws she will cling by her claws
    As it whisks her through the Eurotunnel.
She subsists on cheap cider her French pimps provide her
        To drink with a runcible spoon:
Lundi to dimanche, by the edge of La Manche
    She gets tight by the light of the moon,
        Oh, la lune,
        None too soon,
    How she swoons,
She lies down and she's drowned neath the moon.

## Dodging the 'N Word': Being Black and Female in (Mostly) White, Male Student Halls

## Dyanni Swhyer-Brown (2017)

I stared out of my window at the sunset shining through the gaps between the James Watson Hall and the surrounding buildings. I ducked at one point for fear that a girl outside might think me a peeping Tom. So much for making friends then.

I didn't want to venture out, but I could hear my friend's voice in the back of my head, urging me towards the kitchen. 'Be more sociable!' My food was there and my stomach was growling. It was now or never. I preferred never, but that also meant starvation which I didn't fancy trying. Slowly I pulled the creaky door, each millimetre sending out an echoing screech into the empty hallway.

How could this happen to me? I was used to being the only one, or the 'Tigger' of things. Only child, only friend, only person of colour in the room. Now, I was reduced to the only girl, as well as the only member of an ethnic minority in my university flat. I remembered breaking that news to my mum. She's usually not fazed by me mumbling while trying to beat her Subway Surfers' high score (yes, I am serious. She's addicted). However, saying 'You know I'm the only girl in my halls' flat right?' had her finger hovering over the phone screen and left her running partner, Frizzy, crashing into a brick wall.

'What?' was all she came back with, but I saw everything else in her face.

Her only daughter, smart enough to get into university, surrounded by rampant hormones and dirty, crunchy floors for nine months. If she hadn't boasted to her friends, she would've suggested deferring a year to find alternative housing. But it was too late.

After coming to terms with my imminent departure, Mum made sure I had every variation of Dunn's River seasoning to last me the year. A 'likkle taste of home while you're away' she said, re-sorting the cupboards I had just packed. She would have given me a couple of plantains, but was worried that light-fingered flatmates would mistake them for bananas. I didn't actually think she would leave me here with them. I expected her to move in down the hall and make friends with my flatmates, so I didn't have to. I was a girl's girl. How would I survive nine months with my reflection being the only female company?

No more stalling, I thought, thrusting myself out of the room and tip toeing down the hall. I then spent five minutes galloping between my room and the kitchen door, like a shookhead.

Eventually, I managed to push the kitchen door and not bolt away.

The laughter hit me, before I managed to take everything in. I tried to match faces to Facebook pages, remembering who I met yesterday. The boy with the cheddar grin, who offered to help me with my bags. I refused because I didn't need them thinking I was some limp orchid, with no upper body strength. Was it the lanky, bearded one who caught me Skyping my friend in the cupboard, whilst on a quest for toilet roll? As first impressions come, it was only a matter of time before my weird side emerged.

One of them shook my hand, because a polite wave hello wasn't enough. He asked if he properly pronounced my name, and I had to stifle a snide 'Ha!' It would be some form of sorcery if my name was pronounced correctly the first time around. Loudly and clearly, so all could hear, I revealed the proper way to pronounce it. I even gave a list of acceptable mispronunciations now turned into nicknames like 'Dannie' but not 'Diana'.

Satisfied, I looked for a stool in the furthest corner, taking a homemade cookie out of the tub on the side. It was a piece of home I could replicate, even with a shitty three setting oven. I wasn't paying attention to their conversations. The topic of girls came up at one point, but I couldn't join in. I don't have a girlfriend at Oxford or Cambridge. I have a stuffed dinosaur from Woolworths.

At some point, the ice broke between the five boys as they shared the maddest things they'd done, like accidental school arson or that mad skiing trip they all seemed to have gone on. I was still observing from the safety of my window corner. Dannie Attenborough, thrust from her multicultural life in South London to live amongst melanin – deprived males, in a building named after the discoverer of the DNA structure and a proven racist.

That's when I was blind-sided: as if enjoying the shade beneath a tree housing a sleeping cheetah.

'Can I ask you a question?' one of them directed at me from across the room. I nodded, putting on my friendliest smile.

'I play my music really loud and have a lot of songs with the N-word in them and...' I didn't hear the rest, as my ears set themselves on fire and my eyes rolled to the back of my throat.

Really? REALLY? This was the first full day. Is this how it was going to be for the rest of the year?

I never really understood the concept of 'the burden of representation' before this moment. It was the first time I was aware how much of a minority I truly was. It sounds silly, but I came from a school where white people were the rarity. There were enough white people not to notice a divide but they were still under-represented. Now, I was sat in a room with people who'd never had a proper conversation with a black person before me.

Would they go on to ask if I actually liked chicken and why I wore dreadlocks?

First, stupid question: chicken is universally good. The only reason it has been attached to black people is because we season it. Yes, I need all seven of those seasoning jars, that's why our flat smells so nice when I cook.

Second, I twist my hair. Locs are permanent, these are not. So, if you don't see me all day, I'm either dead or doing my hair. Yes, it does take that long and no, you can't touch it.

Was I now going to be the encyclopaedia for everything black?

They're all still looking this way.

'So, is that okay with you?'

Do I say yes or do I say no? Yes or no? Yay or nay? I don't even use the bloody word. Why has this been put on me?

I looked to the Asian housemate for a supporting glance, but no luck. I should have known he'd be no help. He was the one offering up hand-flipping-shakes!

If I said no, I would be another uptight black girl to them, always finding something to be 'angry at the white man' for. The dandelion scrounging in the garden of freedom and self-expression.

If I said yes, my name would mean 'betrayer' instead of 'precious one'. The phrase 'Dyanni said it was cool' would be used to excuse prejudiced behaviours. If I stayed silent, that would be so much worse. I needed to establish a voice here. Ground rules. I licked my full lips and sighed. They all widened their eyes simultaneously. Were they more scared? I doubt it; there were four of them against little ol' me.

'You can play your music, as long as you're not saying it when you sing along. I don't even say it.'

There. It was done. I set down the law and braced myself for the uproar that followed. Instead, he slowly nodded in agreement and I could breathe again. I had successfully dealt with a racially charged discussion and came out of it unscathed. For years to come, the moment when I, the only female, managed to keep the peace between my unruly male flatmates, without backup, will be remembered amongst students.

The guys seemed to have respected my answer, because conversation swiftly moved onto wanking habits. Yes, with me still in there, and no, they didn't give a damn. They now saw me on their level and I would use it to my advantage, even if that meant suffering through TMI conversations. I even got them to promise to do game night. Me!

If I carried on like this, I could end up being queen. Yes, Dyanni, queen of the Uni-jungle has a pleasant ring to it. However, knowing my luck, I'll end up being Dannie, queen of the park. Not even a nice park. A muddy one, with old crisp packets, lifeless acorn trees and no swings.

## The Nine Muses as To-Do Lists

### Alison Habens (2018)

A list of reasons I wish to write (after George Orwell's famous four):

1. 'Sheer egoism'. Without the word I am nude, nada, nobody, no-go, egoless, see.
2. 'Aesthetic enthusiasm'. I love nouns, verbs, adjectives equally, me.
3. 'Historical impulse'. In a modern world, I want to do something old-school.
4. 'Political purpose'. In a bad world, I need to do something good.

A list of pieces I wish to write (after critic Christopher Booker's 'Seven Basic Plots'):

Rags to Riches – There is straw in my mouth, to spin into gold. No, wait, that's Rumpelstiltskin.

Voyage and Return – On my own Odyssey, I roll up eventually; recognisable, even in disguise, as the hero's wife. Oh, wait, that's Penelope, unpicking her stiches every night to stop the story healing.

The Quest – I keep slipping off for a cigarette. It's as if I can see visions in the smoke, each cloud a quote, each strike enlightening. No, wait, that's The Little Match Girl.

Overcoming the Monster – but I can't go over it, can't go under it, got to go through it; hold on, that's Going on a Bear Hunt. Not known to be a car ride, more of a truck, bedtime story-tellers have thrummed this big boy since the world first turned.

Comedy – any line that makes you laugh but shouldn't.

Tragedy – any line that should make you laugh but doesn't.

Rebirth – about the time when I was a Sumerian scribe and my pen ran out.

A list of three reasons I can't write (after the author Cyril Connolly's well-known saying, 'there is no more sombre enemy of good art than the pram in the hall'):

A. The man-sized perambulator done for drink-driving

B. The teenage one, prone to screaming round corners on two wheels

C. The baby-buggy, fitted in that tight passageway with the others like a Tetris shape. If they all play computer games at the same time, I can get some work done.

Meanwhile, I've squeezed this shrine to the Muses on the hall table:

List of items on my shrine to the Muses: a dusty lyre made of tortoiseshell with nine strings, a feather pen, a globe; comic and tragic masks embellished with sequins; some crumbling laurel leaves (mixed with the car keys and small change) and a parchment scroll. I burn incense in the bedroom, brew tisanes in the kitchen and smoke herbs in the lounge, all to invoke the heightened voices of storytelling. 'Tick': I think it's working. The plot is humming like a spinning-wheel.

List of places I've sourced inspiration previously: philosophers, prophets and psychics; sibyls, sirens and shamans; Narnia, Nirvana, Neverland; Pompey, B & Q. Is this automatic writing or 'do it yourself'?

Tips from top sellers: '"Fool!" said my muse to me' (Philip Sidney – 1583); 'If you get stuck... take a walk, take a bath, go to sleep, make a pie... But don't go to a party' (Hilary Mantel - now). 'The muse's friend, tea doth our fancy aid' (Edmund Waller – 1663) because 'Writing about a writer's block is better than not writing at all' (Charles Bukowski - then).

'Tick': Yes, it's working. Even pram wheels can drive a tale-spinner's ambition. I'm circle-dancing with three times three goddesses of art, music, words; in the smoke-rings with nine classical Greek nymphs wearing floaty tunics. I wish I could say that one was of colour and one was fat and one had only one leg. I'd like to point out the lesbian, the single mother, the one with a tribal tattoo; but they all move the same way. Like, the curve of croissants, pasta twists, spinning pizza bases; the fold of *spanakopita*, whirl of honey, swirl of brown sugar in a *café au lait*. Their palate is toffee to coffee, tan to pain; where they differ is their ages. One of the muses is just a teenager and one is in her twenties; there's a thirty-something, forty-something and fifty-something muse, all dancing in the circle. The seventy, eighty and ninety-year-old muses wear the same translucent togas. Even the geriatric ones have Adriatic blue eyes. And mine, well, it's only ever been the Solent.

As we spin, they sing to me. This is a party. And that is not tea: 'Tick'. One minute, I am sitting, staring at an empty page, a blank screen, wondering what to write there; then comes a whisper, not in my ear but within it, quicker than I can speak, cleverer than I can think. And the next minute I'm typing at top speed to keep up with the lyrics as they disperse like puffs of smoke. Inspiration: it originally meant breathing.

The List of Nine Muses and How Each One Assists Me:

Calliope – Oldest of all, mistress of Apollo, mother of Orpheus, greatest singer-songwriter in the world and the underworld. She's the original thinker up of themes

Clio – Historic, heroic; pricks with wit, from when women had to write with needles instead of pens. She's the first man-handler of memes

Erato – Romantic, erotic; for when women have to write with a penis. She shows me how to spill ink-wet dreams

Euterpe – Metrical, mechanical; the muse of music blows her twin flute with a tune for the multi-tasker. From her I learn how to syncopate plot and sub-plot, harmonise rhythm and rhyme schemes

Terpsichore – Muse of dance, because what writer doesn't want the words to twirl, phrases to *fouette*, and sentences to shimmy; even if we are dancing on our own. From page to stage, in reams

Thalia – It's funny, but once I start seriously calling upon these immortal guides my creativity grows ninefold. I stay up most of the night; and can't remember writing what I wrote, when I scroll back through that nocturnal revision in the morning

Melpomene – It's sad, because the better my work goes, the worse my home life gets. For each brilliant paragraph I pen there's a bitter denouement with someone in person. For every big scene I write, one more insurmountable silence in the flesh

Polyhymnia – It's spooky, how soon fiction starts to overlap fact, at the mountain spring where the inspiring priestesses sat. What I write at night, stoned on the crystal-cut waters, comes true next day; not always in an obvious way, but clear to me

Urania – Muse of Astronomy and Astrology. Spirit mother of Sci-Fi. All who sip from the cyber cup should worship here. Magical, mystical; her favourites and fans support my claim. This is getting supernatural: surely, for my subconscious mind, or where else is that mythical trickle coming from, does not naturally foretell the future, does it...?

List of Prophecies I've Seen Previously:

*Castles with unknown passages are not compatible with my homely muse.* Anthony Trollope. On Sunday, I write how the pram in my hallway leaves for passages new. On Monday, my husband rolls in much later than usual.

*The muse is not an angelic voice that sits on your shoulder and sings sweetly.* Harlan Coben. I write about lyre strings shouting. On Tuesday night, as the document welcomes me where I left off, I tell how the tortoiseshell instrument has blood on its bridge and a broken tooth in its soundbox. On Wednesday he really strums me with it.

*The muses are ghosts, and sometimes they come uninvited.* Stephen King. I don't need to be a writer to recognise this drama is a repeat: his dad beat his mum. How does a character stop doing the only thing it knows how to do?

*I'm not in control of my muse.* Ray Bradbury. Mine's going round and round the Rudmore roundabout, driving drunk and swearing blind I'm the bastard.

'Tick'. Blah blah blah; it might as well be a script in the glovebox. The written version of everything we say, like it's splashed in Hippocrene spring water on the warm dashboard. No, wait; that's Going on a Muse Hunt. Got to catch them all; as if the words we spat were prepared earlier, by the Helicon Nine, on wax tablets.

Basically, he says he's leaving me, because I love nouns, verbs and adjectives better than he; I love Penelope, George Orwell and Hilary Mantel more. He's sodding off which is fine because, according to the seven basic plots, I'm the protagonist and this is my quest.

I write the Bradbury line on Thursday, and on Friday we drive to Bradford via Bury having the fight our muses prescribed, give or take some four-letter words, all the way back to Portsmouth.

'Tick': And the next page is the person he will hit if he doesn't stop the epic effing at me and look at the windscreen. Does reading things make them real?

List of Reasons why I should STOP WRITING:

As the new financial year arrives, Donna Jones and Portsmouth City Council sit down for their annual game of Portsmouthonopoly.

It would appear the board and player tokens have been updated......

**Community chance**

Get the Police to evict a community arts building, then 4 weeks later apply to be a city of culture...

**Will Donna ever..GO?**

Waste 3 million on a rejected combined authority proposal

That no-one but Donna ever wanted...

There is no space for parking in Portsmouth

**Portsmouth**
CITY COUNCIL

**Portsmouthonopoly**

**GO TO JAIL ?**

Spend 50 million on buying commercial property

FOR SALE

No such thing as FREE PARKING in Portsmouth

**Community chance**

Cut 10 million from social care budget then raise Council tax by 2.5 %

PCC collects 14 million

Who is going to tell Donna she cannot play as the old boot anymore? and you cannot build Hotels anymore, only student accommodation blocks......

© Mike Gumbrell, 2018

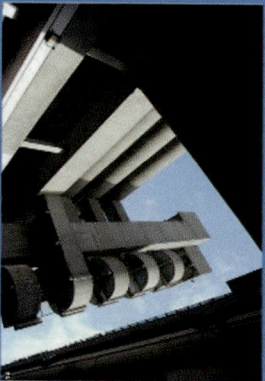

Portsmouth:
Brutalist by Design or
Brutalist by Nature?

© #Higgy, 2018

a politician's open mouth

S/S/S

© Steve Evans, 2018

© Gary Stranger, 2018

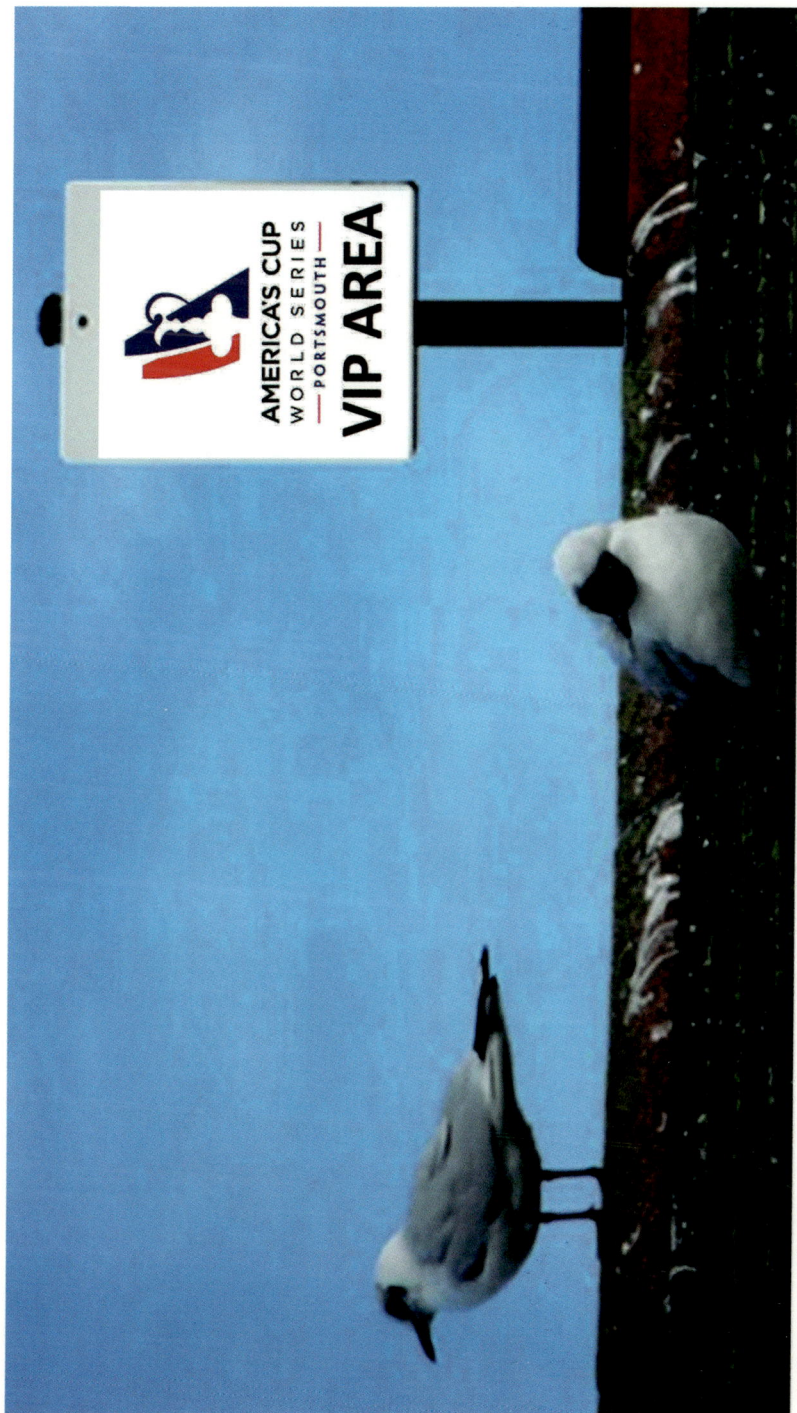

AMERICA'S CUP
WORLD SERIES
— PORTSMOUTH —
VIP AREA

© *Jackson Davies, 2018*

Welcome to *your* council

(opinions from members of the public not welcome)

Welcome to the Civic Offices

A. Plato said there are three kinds of madness; drunkenness, dreaming and possession by the muses. I shriek in hieroglyphs; hell, I cough in cuneiform now.

B. Longfellow said the Helicon of too many poets is not a sunny hillside visited by the Muses, but an old, mouldering house, full of gloom. I scream things from beyond the grave, better conceived with the hot tip of a stake, corrected in ashes with a stick.

C. WB Yeats said what the fairy queen told him, best conceived in Connemara sand, corrected with the hot end of a wand. Lips moving, no sound: 'Be careful, and do not seek to know too much'. I say there is only one question. Does writing things make them real?

Why I'll never stop writing:

The wit behind the lit, Anton Chekov, shouted whoops: 'don't tell me the moon is shining, show me its light glinting on broken glass.' I can see it, full, in the shards of windscreen beside me in the Southsea gutter. Beautiful as the muse mooning.

The manuscript may have gone tits up but even lying down I can still put the ass into classic. My favourites and fans, Homer, Hesiod, Horace, support this claim.

So not dying, I was born for the last instalment. Not golden age Greece, but within halcyon sight of the Isle of Wight.

List of writers who died before they were famous:

1. Emily Dickinson, Kafka, Keats, Herman Melville, Edgar Allen Poe.

2. It is sheer Emily egoism to suppose that my little bit of literary shit will stand for any political Kafka or has, in any sense other than wanking, a purposeful Keats. Who gives two pennorth of poo for the historical impulse of my Melville, or a toss for my professional lifetime of Edgar aesthetic enthusiasm Poe.

3. 'Tick'. Even when nearly dead: life writing. Orwell is my inkwell...

## What Donna Can Learn from Donald

### Sir Eugene Nicks (2017)

Isn't this a whizzo time to be alive, readers? Me old mucker and business partner Donald Trump's doing sterling work as the Lord High Maniac-in-Chief of Ol' Washington Town. How delightful that, right now, his pus-coloured mane is drooping all over the nuclear red button. He'll probably be dribbling over it too, but that's one of many problems of his that I vowed to keep confidential.

I may be the only man on Earth – while it's still here, anyway – who is personal chums with both Donald and Donna, his near-namesake and counterpart over here as leader of Portsmouth City Council. In other words, I'm on excellent terms with the most powerful, egotistical and offensive person in the world... and Donald Trump. And I view this connection as what the Donald might call a 'golden shower opportunity' – I think that's business jargon for something or other – to bring two great minds and two great cultures closer together as we enter an exhilarating new epoch of hope, freedom and tolerance. Or something to that effect.

The other night, Donna and I went for a goblet of benefit claimant's blood at our local public house, the Hypothermic Vagrant. (Incidentally, there was an actual vagrant dying of hypothermia just by the bins outside. He asked me for the price of a cup of tea and I replied, 'I only have fifty-pound notes, old boy.' But I didn't give him one, obviously.)

Anyway, Donna asked me what advice on statecraft she might pass on to Donald via yours truly.

'But my dear lady,' I begged to differentiate. 'Ask not what he can learn from you but what you can learn from he. For Donald has disgraced himself in ways you cannot imagine and stooped to lows that even you have not nightmared of.'

Now humility isn't normally Donna's strong suit... which is why she screamed 'That's nonsense!' in my face. But then she calmed down, the blood working its way to her head, and elected to hear me out. I've been in the political game a long time, recall, and I know it as well as the back of my hand, or even as well as the backhander that plops into my mailbox each morning because I shamelessly blackmail every single elected representative from here to the post-apocalyptic badlands of Wymering.

I reminded Donna that we Portsmouth Tories have done it all – well done them all, more or less: the unemployed, the disabled, the homeless, refugees, old people, young people, tall people, small people. But we haven't been tough enough on the old enemy: the dastardly denizens of Southampton. So, I suggested Donna re-purpose one of Donald's classic raps but along these lines:

'*When Southampton sends its people, they're not sending the best. They're not sending you, they're sending people that have lots of problems and they're bringing those problems with us [sic] They're bringing drugs. They're bringing crime. They're rapists... And some, I assume, are good people.*'

And if that wasn't tough enough, I said to Donna, how about this:

'*I will build a great wall – and nobody builds walls better than me, believe me – and I'll build them very inexpensively. I will build a great, great wall on our western border, and I will make Southampton pay for that wall. Mark my words.*'

Or we may go even further with something like the following:

'*Donna J Trump is calling for a total and complete shutdown of Southamptonians entering Portsmouth, until our city's representatives can figure out what the hell is going on.*'

'But remember,' said Donna, 'that it's not just the social undesirables and the people of Southampton who cause us headaches. We have dangerous political subversives who dare to question our fanatical devotion to austerity.'

'Indeed,' I concurred. 'What about politely borrowing another Trumpian pearl of odium?'

'*Sisters Uncut are crude, rude, obnoxious and dumb – other than that I like them very much.*'

Donna seemed to enjoy that one. I put it to her that, as all Portsmouth Tories know, foreigners – ones even more foreign than people from Southampton – are irredeemably awful. Amongst many many other things, they bring disease. With that in mind, Donna ought to adapt something else Donald's said in the recent past:

'*Stop the Ebola patients from entering Portsmouth. Treat them, at the highest level, over there. Portsmouth has enough problems.*'

We looked out the window at the inclement weather. 'I wish it would improve,' Donna sighed.

I told her that Donald has a spiffing one-liner that she might re-write and make her own:

'*It's freezing and snowing in Portsmouth – we need global warming!*'

'I'm not going out there,' Donna said. 'I might mess up my hair.'

I pointed out to her that Donald also cares deeply about his hair and that this too might be a point of agreement betwixt the pair of them:

'*As everybody knows, but the haters and losers refuse to acknowledge, I do not wear a "wig." My hair may not be perfect but it's mine.*'

It was getting late and time to meet my driver Melania – no relation to Donald or I – in the car park. As we parted company, I asked Donna how she manages to cope with the pressures of her high office.

'When I think I'm right,' she said, 'nothing bothers me.'

Eerie, I thought, Donald said exactly the same thing in 1985. How similar they are. I've yet to see them in the same place at the same time. Have you?

## Old and in the Way?

## Dave Allen (2018)

In January 2018, John Sutherland published a self-described 'polemic' entitled *The War on the Young*; a war he argues is being waged by my generation, 'the baby boomers', against the young people now struggling to pay tuition fees, buy houses and live with the independence my lot enjoyed half-a-century ago.

Of course, not many of us did go to university back then. I got my degree only when I returned to study after more than three years out at work, and it was vocational from the start - teacher training in a College of Education. Many of my 'baby boomer' peers left work at 15 or 16 and went into work, whether apprenticeships or unskilled labour, which left the country to fund something between 5-10% of us to continue studying. More recently, no one has worked out how to keep education free when most youngsters stay on until 18 and these days, almost 50% go on to university. I don't have the answer to that funding conundrum but having spent my working life in schools and universities I have plenty of sympathy.

I still work on projects with young people, though I retired in 2010 as I approached my 61st birthday. I retired following an offer from the university, who wanted people like me off the payroll because we became expensive when the government extended our right to work for ever. There was little chance of that happening with me but they made me an offer I could not refuse and off I went; *retired*. Some of my generation don't like that word: they don't want to feel it's all over, and need to feel busy or 'useful'. But when I use the word retired, I mean simply that I am no longer a wage slave because my income from pensions and savings allows me to live without working for remuneration.

This doesn't apply to everyone. I am middle class, own a pleasant terraced house, an almost new car and have no direct dependents and a modest lifestyle. I have enough to be content. I rarely take holidays, never long ones, and since 2008 never abroad. I can't be bothered with abroad anymore, and I have let my passport expire. I'm not big on shopping either. By comparison with my twenties, these days I don't play football or cricket every weekend – my knees would not like it – nor do I go clubbing two or three times a week, catching the best bands, as I did regularly in the 1960s and 1970s. Of course, that's partly because the bands aren't as good as they were once ... no, sorry, that's not my plan in this piece; these are the things I don't do and defining a lifestyle by its negatives is not productive.

Instead I'd like to try to write something that reconciles old and young, to declare a ceasefire in Sutherland's 'war', or perhaps refute that there is a conflict in the first place.

I mentioned that I still work with young people. These days it's voluntary work and includes tutorial support to university students, but there is one other project that I've found particularly fruitful, and which provides an interesting model of how young and old can work together outside the obvious context of family. Every autumn Portsmouth City Council runs a 60+ Festival aimed principally at retired people and offering a wide range of activities. Because of my involvement in projects related to the history of popular music in Portsmouth, in 2013 they invited me to run a workshop of my choice. What I offered was a morning of reminiscence about music and the so-called 'swinging sixties', from which I hoped to generate new material for display and publication. In truth we just sat around and chatted. It was a good social occasion but, in a way, it epitomised a broader problem: how retired people engage in activities which they enjoy but which have no broader benefits.

Sometimes, that's perfectly fine. If conversation groups combat loneliness and its attendant health problems, I'm all for them. But when I was invited to do something the following year, I wanted participants to be more engaged, even if only for a morning. So, I recruited my pal Denis, with whom I've played music for decades, and we ran a practical skiffle session, recreating that essentially American folk-blues music which was transformed by English teenagers in the mid-1950s, and briefly rivalled rock & roll in the pop charts. Around a dozen people came, some able to play a guitar or ukulele, some happy to bash a washboard or other simple percussion instrument, and all willing to sing along to *Freight Train, Rock Island Line, Putting on the Style* and other favourites from those long-gone days.

They enjoyed themselves and asked for more sessions, at which point the Portsmouth Cultural Trust (created in 2010 by Portsmouth City Council to run the Guildhall) offered us space to meet once a month to entertain each other and learn more songs. A few of the participants' friends joined in and in October 2015 we ran the workshop again, by which time the group had expanded to around 30. I felt it was time to perform, sharpen us up and see how well we were progressing, so we began doing that on Tuesday lunchtimes and now, three-and-a-half years on, the Southsea Skiffle Orchestra (SSO) has around 30 members. We entertain an audience of around 50 or more in the Guildhall every month and have played elsewhere locally, including the Victorious Festival, the King's and New Theatre Royal.

There is nothing terribly innovative about the music of the course, and seeing us is a principally nostalgic experience, enjoyed almost wholly by those who remember the skiffle boom: not only headed around 1957 by Lonnie Donegan, Chas McDevitt and the Vipers, but also by the next generation of British pop musicians including the Beatles, Rolling Stones, Van Morrison and Jimmy Page. The special feature of SSO is our size and age; we are almost certainly the largest skiffle group ever to perform regularly and when added together we clock up over 2,000 years – much older than the Rolling Stones! At most of our gigs we provide song sheets of the choruses, although many of our regular supporters know all the songs by heart – no problems with memory there!

That's a serious point. During the life of SSO, three of our members have suffered serious illness. We have so much fun, that I think when the Orchestra finally ends it won't be due to irreconcilable musical differences, but because we'll no longer be fit enough, perhaps not even around, to perform. In the meantime, I'd argue everything we do ourselves and with our regular audiences is helping to keep us emotionally and intellectually alert – at no cost to the National Health Service.

This brings me to the economics of such an enterprise – what is the cost? At a simple level, we purchase and maintain our instruments, get ourselves to gigs, produce the song sheets and maintain at least a basic level of 'marketing' – not a term in common use in the days of the 2i's Coffee Bar! We don't take any money from the gigs; even a fee of £150 would leave each of us with no more than a fiver, so we do a couple of other things. The simplest is that we play for nothing, usually for charity fundraisers – the biggest and best of which was at Christmas 2017 when we joined with other bands at the Square Tower to raise around £2,000 for the 'Help the Homeless' project at St Simon's Church. On other occasions, we take a small fee (£30 or £40) and add this to the voluntary collections we make after our Guildhall gigs. Most of this goes towards supporting young people performing showcase gigs at the same venue, which allows them to offer free entrance, while providing payment for the young musicians.

We've also recently become involved with local schools – one head teacher brought some of his junior school pupils to watch us at the Guildhall and they were intrigued by the washboards, kazoos, harmonicas and tea-chest bass; not instruments that feature regularly in whatever might be the modern equivalent of *Top of the Pops*. They particularly enjoyed the idea of making music without 'real' instruments, and especially liked the 'bottles' (jugs).

We also shared a fun day with older pupils from a comprehensive school in Cowplain. They have a large school band called Jukebox run by their music teacher Sue Dobbyn with whom I play in another band, Scarlet Town. Jukebox and the Southsea Skiffle Orchestra performed on the main Guildhall stage, they with a mixture of contemporary 'pop' and older funky classics by Aretha Franklin and Stevie Wonder. Intrigued by our pre-historic instruments and sound, they asked Sue whether they might add instruments like harmonicas and kazoos to their sound. As usual we held a collection at the end of the free event, and we sent them back to school with around £130 to contribute to their music-making.

Far from being any conflict between the generations, we are finding ways of bridging gaps through the sharing of creative practices – in the case of 'Jukebox', very much a two-way sharing.

There are many more such projects and activities happening around Portsmouth, some emerging through the work of students at the University, others through community-funded activities, if they're fortunate enough to find funding. One is the Urban Vocal Group who work with 'less-advantaged' local young people and through their singing workshops and *Breaking Through* project developing the young stars of the future including Josh, Beth, Faye, Ellie & Livvy.

I have a suspicion that music is particularly powerful in such projects but it could equally be writing, visual art, theatre, dance or any of the arts. I recently worked with a group of students who formed a company for an assessed project called 'Minder', which aimed to support mental health by using the arts as a catalyst for conversations about anything and everything. A different group I know of are exploring the arts as a means of reflecting on the daily experience of living with the reporting and *possibility* of acts of terrorism, impacting on 'ordinary' people in 'ordinary' situations. In both cases, there are things I could share with young people from a different perspective. For example, when I was their age (nearly fifty years ago) there were far fewer instances that I was aware of mental ill health problems experienced by my peers; and while there were instances of terrorism in mainland Britain, relating to the problems in Ireland, they did not seem to impinge on everyday life in the same way as we find today.

Because of my career and interests I find it easy to get engaged in such activities – people ask me, and I guess I have a reputation for saying yes. In sharing my experiences here, I wonder how can we enable more people of my generation to share their life experiences, skills and knowledge with younger people – not only for their benefit, but also for ours, particularly those of us with less energy, and fewer sparks of excitement these days? My title is taken from a band that was an offshoot of the Grateful Dead, but I'd rather we third-agers might be the Grateful Living, and Old *Along* the Way, in partnership with young people who are no foes of mine.

## Robin Cook and My Part in His Resignation

### Rosy Bremer (2018)

In November 2002, the tragedy that was the Bush-Blair war in Iraq and its aftermath had yet to occur. There had been previous onslaughts, invasions, bombings and punitive sanctions but the unjust war on a dodgy pretext hadn't happened yet.

I was, at that time, working for a charity with an office (a room) in the former Portsmouth Housing Association building opposite St Mary's Church. I could both walk to work and stop at a charity shop on the way home to buy a size 14 white acrylic jumper when needed. The day before a die-in at Whitehall protesting the planned war in the Middle East was one occasion I needed to buy a size 14 white acrylic jumper. When I got home I chucked a half-full can of red paint at it.

Then I got up the next day and chucked a bit more red paint at myself, and put the jumper on top of three other jumpers and a waterproof coat. The idea was that I should look like a right bloody mess, and a right bloody mess I looked too. I looked so much of a bloody mess that, when I was walking to the train station to go to London, a woman stopped her car, got out and asked if I was okay. She seemed most relieved when I told her about the rationale behind looking like the walking wounded, and she agreed with the anti-war argument.

When I got to Whitehall I found a large group of people wrapped in bandages, placards and whatnot. We dutifully lay down in as ungainly an arrangement of people opposed to war as possible and looked forward to Whitehall grinding to a halt. Cars slowed and weaved for a bit, the police went through a short spell of ditheryness and then decided that the way to manage the ungainly lying-down people appearing like a huge outdoor First Aid lesson was to shut half the road and let things carry on as normal.

'Carry on as normal?' I said to someone horizontal on the tarmac next to me. 'I haven't bought a several-sizes-too-big-for-me jumper, chucked paint at it, got up early, analysed the case for war, spoken to several Iraqi refugees about their view of the threat of military action, lived through and opposed previous attacks on Iraq only for everything to carry on as normal when we've specifically set out to stop things carrying on as normal'.

It was also quite cold and boring, lying in the London road as buses and lorries lumbered past. So, I got up and set off along Whitehall, looking for a corridor of power into which I could burst forth with some incisive and non-violent opinions. My preferred choice was the War Rooms, which were just asking for a visit from a peace activist but they seemed to be quite well-guarded. Supremely un-guarded, though, were the doors to the Cabinet Office. Nothing I like more than supremely un-guarded doors to corridors of power and what better to do than strolling calmly through such doors?

Into the Cabinet Office I strolled, enlightening all those I met therein with my on-the-spot assessment of the planned course of action vis-a-vis Iraq. The police turned up fairly quickly after I disclosed my fears. They turned up with all traces of earlier dithering quite vanished. This was quite clearly a situation that called for some decisive action; decisive action in the form of two policemen picking me up, carrying me out of the Cabinet Office and plonking me onto the pavement, like a sack of activist maris pipers.

By now it was lunchtime and I joined my recumbent traffic-busting friends. I was quite taken with the idea of the Cabinet Office's open-door policy and went to tell the lying-in-the-road contingent that they might be better off where I'd been earlier. Nobody wanted to come with me, though, so I set off again from whence I'd been ejected.

Again, the Cabinet Office's big, posh doors yawned wide open saying as they did so 'Bring me your tired, your anti-war, your cuddled masses yearning to breathe peace and we will call some coppers to chuck them out'. It was the same performance as before and I again reported back that the Cabinet Office's doors were still open and it was still a good place to go and stop the work of government planning a disastrous war.

Still nobody wanted to do anything other than lie flat on the road (nowt so queer as activists missing the moment) which left just me, myself and I to go back for a third time. This time the good old London bobbies were really on the ball. After expelling me for a third time they took some really radically decisive action, and shut the doors.

This left me on the steps of the Cabinet Office with about five police people and two security guards in a strange but effective blockade. I had completely forgotten to have any lunch in all the to'ing and fro'ing so I started eating some celery when a small man in a suit with a slightly displeased expression appeared in front of me. As I was on the steps of the Cabinet Office I was in the novel position (for a woman of roughly 152 cms) of looking down on someone.

'Ah, Mr Cook,' I said nonchalantly nibbling celery, 'I was waiting to speak to you. A lot of people in the UK think the planned war in Iraq is immoral and unlawful.' I waited for a reaction, as I looked into his blue eyes. There wasn't much sign of a reaction so having said what I wanted to say, I stepped aside to let him in.

I only had to wait another four months for Robin Cook's reaction: 'I cannot support a war without international agreement or domestic support' began his resignation speech. It went on to be one of the most graceful and most dignified resignation speeches and it forensically demolished every aspect of the case for war.

It was all the more surprising a resignation, as Cook had previously supported bombing and harshly sanctioning the Iraqi people. He had also been one of the architects of the 'humanitarian intervention' policy in Kosovo and the former Yugoslavia.

Something had happened to change his mind; something like the British people in many different ways speaking truth to power. It just so happened that I spoke truth to power in a paint-spattered acrylic top and a stick of celery in my hand.

## Ferries at Southsea

### Stephanie Norgate (2016)

At George's, we see the ferries coming in,
huge trays of light buoyant in the dark blue evening,
floating out of the night towards the palm trees,
towards the young drunk spraycanning the pavement,
his words sputtering away. We watch the ferries,
coming in, their unsteady flickerings like poems,
freighted with the dead, the living and the refugees,
carrying those who don't mind the long way over,
lotus-eaters or dreamers or souls returning,
lit up and floating, like lights themselves,
like the strings of lights that curve and stretch
along Clarence Parade, lighting us to our cars
when we leave at midnight. Soon those night-travellers
will disembark too, dragging their rucksacks
down slipways, smuggling their talents through customs,
dreaming firm ground under their feet,
dreaming, as they try to enter a new berth,
of their children in safe houses
in quiet streets where nights can be dull,
and the only flash is the flash of a car's light
on the elder flowers, crowded and sultry.

## 'HITLER THE MAN': Eighty Years of Portsmouth News Bigotry

### Tom Sykes (2018)

It's difficult to think of a pundit more rabid and blinkered than Katie Hopkins, but Clive Smith of the Portsmouth *News* comes close. Over the last year or so he has praised Donald Trump, called for the doubling of the number of Formula One 'walk-on' girls and demanded the streets of Portsmouth be 'cleared of homeless' because 'Hobo Bob and his flea-ridden mutt' doesn't show our city in a good light.

In December 2015, *Star & Crescent* reported on the widespread anger caused by Smith's ridiculing of depression: 'Why everyone needs to have a label lately is beyond me. Bipolar seems to be all the rage at the moment.' At no point in his piece does Smith think critically about the broader social reasons for mental distress. 'From time to time,' he writes simplistically, 'we all get dealt a bad hand – some more than others.' Instead he reinforces lazy, outdated stereotypes about men rather than encouraging them to confront and address their problems – an unhelpful stance bearing in mind that suicides amongst young males in Britain have increased by 15 per cent in the last 35 years. 'Everyone knows men don't talk about things,' he blusters. 'The way some are dripping on these days is frankly embarrassing. So buck up boys and quit the moaning. It's getting boring.'

Phrases like 'dripping on' and 'buck up' have a curiously archaic feel. This is apt given that, over the last eighty or so years, other News journalists have expressed reactionary views often out of step with the values of their times – though, in comparison, they make Smith's outbursts seem almost cuddly.

Amidst extensive News coverage of Enoch Powell's notorious 'Rivers of Blood' speech and its aftermath, the paper's editorial of 22 April 1968 asserts, 'Whether we agree with Mr. Powell or not, he was doing no more than expressing the feelings of British people who see in the Race Relations Bill not only a threat to their own living standards but ultimately, loss of control over their own destinies. Public feeling is not so much a colour prejudice but a rebellion against the provisions of a Bill which, amongst other things, seeks to force British people by law to do what they instinctively do not want to do.'

The cunning caveats, 'Whether we agree with Mr. Powell or not' and 'Public feeling is not so much a colour prejudice', hardly soften the profoundly racist argument that follows: that the Race Relations Bill – the most important endeavour in our legal history to extend fundamental human rights to BAME Britons – goes against the essential instincts of white Britons.

An apologist might say that the editor of *The News* in 1968 was simply echoing the views of most right-thinking people. But that would be a selective reading of history. Tony Benn, then a Labour cabinet minister, said after Powell's intervention, 'The flag of racialism which has been hoisted in Wolverhampton is beginning to look like the one that fluttered 25 years ago over Dachau and Belsen.'

It wasn't just key figures in the Labour government who were appalled. Conservative leader Edward Heath – no far-left firebrand – promptly sacked Powell from his shadow cabinet. Even the solidly establishment *Times* newspaper accused Powell of making an 'evil speech ... This is the first time that a serious British politician has appealed to racial hatred in this direct way in our postwar history.'

Powell was also an unswerving sexist. Long after the 'Rivers of Blood' affair he said in a TV interview 'women didn't exist' for him during his time studying at Cambridge University. 'I didn't think they would approach advanced learning in the same mood or manner as a man would. The analytical faculties are underdeveloped in women.' Proving that he hadn't reformed his views in 85 years, Powell made these comments shortly before his death in 1998.

A similar sentiment can be found in a 6 September 1972 *News* column entitled 'Merely Male', in which one Arnold Chilton ascribes poor female driving to 'women [being] constitutionally incapable of telling their left hand from their right. It's just one of a number of disabilities they suffer from.' At the height of the second wave of feminism movement, such chauvinism came from the pen of a professional writer employed by a serious newspaper.

Women's liberation was just one aspect of human progress some News contributors resisted during the 1960s and '70s. 'The machinery and practice of family planning', so argues an editorial from 24 May 1968, will result in 'immorality encouraged by permissive attitudes, lack of parental example and guidance, and the disappearance of self-discipline.'

By 20 September 1972, long after the unbanning of *Lady Chatterley's Lover* and a general liberalisation of British attitudes to sex, another editorial calls for 'a more broadly based board of film censors and a much stricter control of sex education in schools.'

We need to go back a little further into the history of *The News* to find even nastier postures. It is widely agreed that apartheid – a system under which a minority of white South Africans subjugated, terrorised and occasionally massacred the black majority in that country – was not one of humanity's lovelier achievements. There was international opposition to apartheid from its very inception, although you wouldn't know it from a page-long News op-ed from 14th March 1951 that justifies the programme by invoking odious racist stereotypes:

'From this [racial] admixture comes the "skolly" – the half-animal, half-civilized gangster of Cape-Town. He lives in District Six, an appalling area of shacks on one of the lower slopes of Table Mountain. He adopts, openly and truculently, his uniform of three-quarter length baggy trousers, with cap pulled down over the eyes. He is never without a knife ... The "skolly" has made District Six the most dangerous area of any city in the world ... The Cape, in brief, is a human cesspit.'

The writer of this screed, 'Paulalim' (meaning, somewhat pretentiously, 'little by little' in Latin), goes on to defend racial segregation in crude biological terms disturbingly reminiscent of Nazi propaganda:

'There comes a time in every Cape Town youngster's life when Dad takes him along to a museum where large glass cases contain waxwork figures of the original inhabitants of the Cape ... To be frank it is an anthropological Chamber of Horrors ... The stunted, debased figures offer hardly a suggestion of man as the European conceives his species. When the Cape-Town father has shown that lot to young Johnny he can rest assured that the boy is unlikely to become an airy critic of the miscegenation laws.'

Clearly, 'Paulalim' had learned little about the dangers of racism from World War II, which had ended but six years before.

Throughout the 1930s, a number of articles in *The News* voiced concerns about the rise of European fascism. Unfortunately, a number of others voiced sympathy for it. In discussing the relative merits of Adolf Hitler and Benito Mussolini, *The News*' 'Special Correspondent' writes on 17 December 1930, 'Mussolini is by far the more spectacular and impressive figure of the two ... The moment he dies there will be disintegration and the old party strife will begin all over again.'

Likewise, he adds, 'take away Hitler and you destroy the new movement among German youth.'

More problematic is what appears to be a neutral news report on Hitler's election manifesto dating from 2 March 1932 with this headline: 'HITLER THE MAN To Lead Germany to Liberty!' The words are not placed between quote marks, implying that this affirmative, even upbeat statement is a creation of the writer's or sub-editor's, not an excerpt from the manifesto or any other source.

After President Hindenburg had appointed Hitler as Chancellor of Germany following two inconclusive elections, *The News* grew more favourable to the Nazis. An editorial from 2 May 1933 praises the new regime's strategies for solving unemployment and high interest rates: 'This is fine! Everybody at work, and work for everybody. Some persons will be saying that it is time we had a Hitler here, just as they used to sigh for a Mussolini.' Later on, the byline-less author uses the adjective 'admirable' to describe 'the part about work' in one of Hitler's recent addresses.

The article makes no mention of the already dreadful oppression happening in Germany at the time. Earlier that same year the Nazis had passed laws denying Jews the right to certain jobs, a proper education and full citizenship. Other legislation had effectively abolished democracy, banned the press and rescinded the right to a fair trial. Violent street assaults on political opponents had become commonplace.

But for this particular News journalist, none of these outrages could take the shine off whatever Hitler was achieving with his new labour policies.

Again, we can't excuse such opinions as just following 'community standards'. It is true that many elements of the British establishment of the period had fascist leanings, Lord Rothermere's *Daily Mail* newspaper notable amongst them. But many journalists and public intellectuals of the early 1930s – from Isaac Deutscher to CLR James to George Orwell – were strongly critical of Hitler's Germany and Mussolini's Italy. For whatever reason, none of them ever wrote for *The News*.

None of the above is to suggest that, as Roy Greenslade has said of *The Mail*'s approval of Hitler and Oswald Mosley (leader of the British Union of Fascists in the 1930s), *The News* 'is somehow tainted goods in its modern form.' But maybe there are lessons to be learned today about thinking carefully before publishing knee-jerk, one-sided commentaries that play into the hands of bigots and reactionaries.

## Red Balloons

### Christine Lawrence (2018)

She was beautiful, there was no doubt about it and when she'd raised her glass to him, his heart had nearly burst. They'd met on a summer night, on the beach in Southsea. I know, it's not that romantic: crunching along a pebbled beach is not quite the same as the sand between your toes. Still they hadn't cared, they only had eyes for each other.

How quickly things can change. Summer was over, taking the romance along with it. There has to be more to a relationship, he thought, than a tumble on the shingle. Sitting in front of the telly alone on a stormy winter night wasn't the same: his love of football meant nothing to her and her desire to go to the theatre just left him cold.

Her artistic friends sneered at him whilst his mates down the pub just pissed her off - he'd watched her shudder as they talked, every other word beginning with an F, their conversation obviously jarring against her sensitivities.

He wondered what they'd ever seen in each other, now the nights were dark and the days so short. He found himself drawn again to the sea front, trying in vain to grasp back what it was they'd had as he looked out to the Island, the rain dripping down his neck. Where do you go from here? he wondered.

Oh, it was good in the beginning, but now she was making so many demands on him, on his time, and asking for money in that whining voice of hers. What did the woman need anyway? He'd given her everything she'd asked for and she had been so pliable at first, allowing him to do anything to her that he wanted. She'd liked it, laughing and smiling at him in that beguiling way she did.

It was the rise and fall of the sea that had lulled him to love someone again, made him lower his guard. The sea had to be the answer to set him free again.

He began his plan.

His favourite place, the funfair, was dark and shuttered against the winter storms but he still loved to walk there, especially at night. He didn't even need to break into the boarded area as he still had the key they'd given him back in the summer. He was familiar with every part of the grounds, empty now of all but memories, shingle and a dried-up starfish the last high tide had washed over the breakwaters.

He stood for a moment under the Wild Mouse, its frame soaring high into the night sky, beams creaking against the elements. Just looking up made him feel so light and full of power. He knew every little part of this place and all that was in it. The summer months he'd spent working here maintaining the rides was coming to fruition at last. It didn't take him long to prepare what he'd planned and soon he was hurrying along to the pier where he'd agreed to meet her for a Valentine's Day surprise.

She sat at the bar. He swallowed his leaping heart.

'Another new dress,' he said and smiled into her eyes. 'You look beautiful.'

She raised her glass to him, the blood red of the wine matching the colour of her dress. 'Thank you,' she leaned towards him and whispered, 'Happy Valentine's Day. Are you having a drink?'

'Maybe later. But first, I've planned a surprise.'

Her stiletto heeled shoes weren't really the thing to wear for walking along the promenade, and she complained all the way.

'Don't worry, we're nearly there and it will be worth it.' He held her close to him as they stumbled along.

As they turned into the fairground he could feel her shivering next to him but as soon as he'd opened the door into the enclosure, she began laughing. Twenty, forty, fifty red balloons were floating around the Wild Mouse, too many to count.

'You're crazy!' she cried into the night as she turned to kiss him on the lips. 'You've done this for me? Are we going on the ride?'

'Just you,' he said. 'You know I hate heights, but I wanted to do something that you would appreciate more than anything, and I know you will love this.'

He watched as she climbed aboard, he checked that the seat belt was securely in place, then went into the box to start the motor. Slowly, the car moved off. He climbed down and his eyes followed the path of the car carrying his love: it laboured up to the top of the ride, turned the corner at the summit and listened to her screams as it sped down the first descent. He watched as it climbed again, heard the creaking of the wheels on the track, saw it pick up speed on the straight at its highest point and smiled as he heard her screams again as the car hit the bend and flew into the night above the sea.

He didn't even hear the splash.  The night was too stormy.

It took quite a while to untie all the red balloons as one by one, he released them into the winter sky.

## Japan Wonderland

### Emily Priest (2018)

*Itadakimasu*

'Itadakimasu,'[1] I chime as I snap apart my chopsticks and stab them into the sticky belly of rice.

My father copies, 'Itti-kaki-mas-oo', snapping his chopstick in half and biting the soft head off his heap of food.

We don't say much for a few minutes but muse at one other and make a series of groans and grins. I pick up a moist clump and dunk it into a small, round dish. The pristine balls of inflamed rice quickly become a rich, reddish brown as it contacts the sauce, absorbing the soy. I place it in my mouth and nod and moan as the tanginess erupts.

Fifteen hours ago, we were eating McDonald's burgers in Heathrow airport, not yakiniku[2] in a Shibuya tavern. We were waiting for our 11 o'clock flight to Tokyo. As a researcher my father has always been invited to countless countries to attend conferences. Normally he goes alone but, this time, he brought me along. I have always adored Japan and dreamed of going and, on many occasions, have voiced these aspirations to my father. Somewhere along the line he must have listened because here we are, clumsily eating with chopsticks, on a trip that may be work for him, but is pure pleasure for me.

Several more plates and bowls are placed around us. They are all patterned with deep blue and murky splatters to mimic traditional Edo[3] period wares. I pull one bowl close to me, pluck up some of the shredded cabbage and chew on it for a sweet crunch. Then, I take some meat from one of the larger plates and drop it on the wide, steaming tray before us. A seductive crackle breaks the silence as the once red slice of steak becomes dark grey. And then, seconds later, deep brown.

We eat for some time, mixing the soy, rice, cabbage and meat and then order more plates and two glasses of sake. Both my father and I sip on the saucers, like egg cups, and savour the creamy, bitter liquid.

---

1    Translation: 'Let's eat'.
2    A Japanese variation of Korean barbecue.
3    The period between 1603 and 1868.

We fry some onions and liver too as our cheeks begin to glow a childish pink. We sway, cross-legged on the green tatami[4] mats. As we finish, we leave five crisp thousand-yen notes on the wooden table.

'Arigatou gozaimasu,'[5] two servers yell out to us in deep male voices. They give wide grins and are dressed yellow-stained aprons.

I mimic them, bowing slightly.

'Aggi-cat-oh...,' my father tries, '...gozzy-mas.'

Embarrassed, I shove his large, drunken body out of the door. His forehead slaps against the red patterned flags that hang overhead as he reluctantly enters the cool, night air.

It is only 9 o'clock in the evening but already, even in the summer, it has grown dark in the city. The towering high-rises and offices become dark blue and black around us. But, the city will not be asleep, not just yet as the noise from Tokyo's landscape surrounds us excitedly. Karaoke, clubs, Pachinko stalls[6], ramen chefs and supermarkets have their own role to play in the chaos of the night-time street. Singing can be heard from within walls. Servers, in more white aprons and paper hats, loudly thank patrons and serve them with steaming bowls of thick noodles. Elderly men drowsily hunch over machines that they relentlessly feed money. From outside, you can watch their silhouettes push buttons, pull levers and check for any winnings.

We walk up the high street as strangers and cars manically zip past. Few passers-by notice us, two wandering foreigners, but the rest continue, drunk or carrying countless shopping bags. Their bodies are illuminated pink, red and orange underneath advertisements and shop signs. A group of young girls catch my attention. They laugh amongst themselves, flaunting their newest jewellery and phone charms. They wear dresses, frills and ribbons, with bows in their hair and colourful fox tails clipped to their bags. One notices me and nervously tells her friend and points in my direction. Just as they look new and exciting to me in their gowns and one-pieces, I seem odd in to them my shorts and tank top. Another girl widens her eyes at the designs on my leg. Even if common in western society, tattoos are still an unusual, mostly shunned, fashion accessory in Japan. In fact, they are symbols associated with the Yakuza[7].

I continue through Shibuya, I wonder what those girls, with their

---

4 Traditional Japanese flooring made from rice straw.
5 Translation: 'Thank you very much'.
6 A mechanical game used for gambling.
7 Organised crime syndicate originating from Japan.

childish make up and knee-high socks, thought of me. Were they intrigued? Curious? Or perhaps scared? Is my blatant parade of Western culture an offence to those Japanese girls?

I begin to question what it really means to be a traveller as we take a left and slip into the alleyways that wind around hotels and bars. The city centre dissolves into flats and houses, street signs and shrubbery. The overhead lamps guide us, hanging in the darkness like will-o'-the-wisps. They entice us further into this wonderland.

## Akihabara

A short, 30-minute journey on the Ginza line, towards Asakusa, takes me to another nightscape with even more vibrancy and culture. Akihabara, the mecca of anime[8], may seem like another bustling, Japanese street but don't let it fool you. These people are not your every-day workers but fans of Japan's biggest sub-culture. The buildings are not offices but rather towering, light speckled shops, twenty to thirty storeys high, overflowing with peculiar merchandise.

Tourists flock here, locals too, and they swarm around store entrances and zip between each other with fists filled with bag handles and loose change. On the street, there are a few girls, handing out leaflets and holding signs, dressed in maid outfits and cat costumes, approaching men with starry eyes and grinning faces. One, with small black ears and a tail, wears a puffed-out period style dress with knee-high socks. Her shoes are polished and childish and at the edge of her sleeves and skirt stream bows, ribbons and frills. She meows sweetly at potential customers as she hands them a sheet of paper and directs them to a nearby building.

Despite her sign forbidding pictures, I sneakily take a photograph before hurrying off to one of the many stores. Inside, the lights gleam a fluorescent white and there are more bodies pressed against one another in small rooms crowded with goods. A few teenagers walk past with arms filled with volumes and a couple of men, a bit older than myself, huddle around phone charms and keyrings, discussing which one to buy their girlfriends – I assume.

Each floor holds a different form of merchandise with manga[9] on the bottom floor and an array of Lolita[10] fashion on the top. Here, you

---

8   Japanese term for hand-drawn or computer animation.
9   Comics created in Japan.
10  Fashion subculture originating from Japan based on Victorian and Edwardian attire.

find petticoats, floral dresses and oversized clip-on bows. There is everything you could imagine with stickers and stationery, wigs and dolls. This shop I have found myself in reveals itself to be an Aladdin's cave of a subculture simultaneously shunned, admired and fetishised.

I recognise some of the characters and quickly fill my palms with t-shirts, keyrings and a 1/6 scale figurine of Konata[11] from Lucky Star. I find her on the top shelf, just out of my reach, with her pouting face protected behind sheets of plastic. I reach and stretch and finally she falls. I catch the box and turn it over to reveal the schoolgirl, dressed in a white and pink outfit, hand on her hip and the other pointing into the air. Like an eager toddler, I present her to the cashier. Proudly, I press a clump of crushed up notes and coins into the elderly man's hand.

In another shop, with less people, I find myself enviously staring at skirts and shirts, stroking fabrics and picking at layers. There are school girl outfits, pristine and pressed, as well as Lolita sets I have once seen on the internet and fallen in love with. The detail and novelty had made me swoon and I envied the girls who dressed like dolls in them with pretty bows and childish toys. I wanted to be as cute as them, like real life anime characters, and I wondered if us girls strive to become children again – adorable and naïve. Do we want to be looked after like babies and go back to a time where we had no adult responsibilities? Or do we strive for perfection and to become dolls? Do we secretly want to be put back into our boxes, protected by plastic, where men can only gaze at and love us from a distance, rather than grope us with fumbling fingers?

I drag myself away as, even if I could afford the tens of thousands of yen price tags, those perfect dresses cannot be so easily transferred to my own culture. In Japan, girls who dress in such apparel are deified. From ages seven to sixteen, girls wear cutesy fashion, dance and sing in pastels and sparkles. They are called 'idols' and are adored by girls and boys and men and women. Japanese girls strive to meet the purest beauty standards yet, when you travel West, more mature and salacious styles are preferred. You would not find a lack of skin with dark make-up, fishnets and cleavage popular in the Land of the Rising Sun. Such adornments of sexuality are dismissed and virginity is worshipped.

I wander more and pass maid and butler cafés where patrons not only eat animal-shaped pastries and desserts, but swoon over

---

11   A female anime protagonist with long blue hair.

attractive members of staff also. Large advertisements tell you where to go, down or upstairs, to meet a maître d' who takes a sizeable entry fee. The females are, of course, adorable in both image and personality

'Yokoso goshijinsama,'[12] they sweetly chime to you in pinafores and stockings.

The men, more revered and charming, nod in suits and bow to female customers.

They serve you thoroughly and kindly, and the food is decorated with the utmost care. You can order a strawberry cheesecake for 8,000 yen with layers of soft yellow sponge, fresh cut strawberries, oozing whipped cream and a decorative signature, made with sauce, on the side. The signature varies from restaurant to restaurant with some establishments writing the customer's name, a little message or a drawing of a cat. There is entertainment too, dancing and singing mainly, and many customers leave hours later, drunk on excitement and liquor.

After I sample this lifestyle, I stand in the centre of the colourful chaos, between shops and novelty cafes, with my hands filled with bags and my stomach with sweets. The flashing lights and adverts cluster overhead into a cloud of orange and blue lights that intoxicate me further. Drunken on the unique flare of 'Nippon',[13] I feel that perhaps I am dreaming. Or, have I just fallen too far into the rabbit hole?

I find myself addicted to this world, so new and strange, and all the colour and adventure it promises. The dresses, cartoons and people are all moreish delectable treats of an ephemeral culture I will never be able to take home in my suitcase.

---

12  Translation: Welcome Master.
13  A formal Japanese term for Japan.

## Wabi Sabi
### Richard Peirce (2018)

On my way back from the gym
I set down my bike on the beach
above the watermark
where the spring tides
had abandoned their debris.

A pause - after the lists, notes, spreadsheets
of the morning's self-inflicted tasks
and the drab, pop-blaring TV screen of the fitness suite,
turgid love songs - the grunting, the sweating,
the clank and whirr of the machines.

Lying out on the pebbles
I shuffled my arse to create a hollow,
backpack for a pillow.
The sparkle on the water hurt my eyes
but drew me to its beauty.

The pounding breakers
pushed and dragged the stones,
slowing my heartbeat.
The sun burned through the chill air -
settled on the leaf-fall of my life.

*Author's note: In Japan, wabi sabi was originally associated with sadness and loneliness. Today, it usually refers to a simple and modest lifestyle; one which is peaceful, balanced and in tune with nature.*

## Dr Manfratton: An Origin Story

### Jon Crout (2015)

It is 1992. It is Fudger's birthday, and we are sat in his shed, hiding from his mum. She's got the hump because he re-enacted Anderton's goal at Highbury in her lounge and broke her clock. We've got two cans of Fosters, and plan to lay low for an hour until she goes to bingo, so that we can sneak off and meet a couple of girls at the Poly. By meet, I mean he's heard that they'll be there, and he fancies his chances. We end up staying in the shed all night because that stupid latch is broken, and if it gets closed too hard, it jams more solid than Chris Burns' forehead. Only Mr Packer knows how to jiggle it just right from the outside to get it open again. Summer is almost here, but it still gets bloody cold at night. Fudger is the first one to crack, and he asks if he can cuddle in. His dad finds us the next morning in an awkward embrace on the floor, his eldest child spooning his best friend with an unhealthily stained tarpaulin draped over both. I am clutching Mr Packer's secret reading matter in one hand, and his son's right hand in the other. The thing we are told off for the most is relieving ourselves in the corner, too close to the fledgling tomato plants. I decline all offers of salad when round there for dinner that year. It will be eight more years until the accident.

I see the past ahead of me and the future behind me, catching glimpses of all that was, and might be, mirrored in every surface. I walk sideways through time, sometimes spinning round and moving my head from side to side. Occasionally I jump up and down. The idea that time is linear is one I had never even thought of, in that past before all was changed, yet in an instant I can synthesise a PowerPoint presentation that makes clear what a ludicrous notion this is.

At a match in 2008 we are celebrating a belated centenary, actually marking 110 years, another chronal absurdity. I am on the cover of the programme. I pick this programme up from the dust of the old stadium ruins many years later. I look at the dirt stained picture of this unlikeliest of mascots and let it fall from my fingers. At half time of that same match, a steward explains that they want a word in private. There have been complaints. Some people are unhappy at their view being partially obscured by a big blue man. There are unsubstantiated reports that my aura is somehow affecting the taste of the pies. I should be able to influence the molecular composition of these with just a thought. There does not seem any point. I can sense a shift in how this world is put together. In the future, I let the old programme fall from my fingers, and I look enigmatically up at the sky, even though there is no one around to see me pose. Before it hits the dust once more, I am very far away. In Farlington.

Fudger got very excited about the millennium. He bought loads of tacky merchandise from the internet, and he became almost obsessed with how society would survive following the near apocalyptic effects of the bug. It is the week before New Year's Eve 1999. We are in the local, and he is very drunk. It is making his explanations to the young ladies at the bar as to how he came by his nickname unnecessarily complicated. Plus, I don't really think they care. He gets very angry with me for pointing out that the millennium proper doesn't actually happen until next year, partly because he thinks I am being pedantic just to annoy him, and also because he is worried that I will seem more interesting, and therefore more desirable, to the objects of his own affection. He is wrong on all counts. We go back to his mum and dad's on our own that night. I try to explain to him that I am pedantic because that's just the way I am, but when I look up, I realise that he has fallen asleep in the armchair. He will wake up with chilli sauce on his chin and chicken between his teeth. I turn off Alien and start to watch the recording of that night's *Match of the Day*.

About a year before they devoted an entire issue to me, New Scientist ran a small article about the discovery of a new type of radiation. Rather than behave as a wave or a particle, these packets of energy come into existence, seemingly from nowhere, as quantum star-bursts that explode and implode simultaneously, framed in four dimensions by arcing spherical slivers of the same ethereal force, that exists everywhere and nowhere before disappearing in a way that is impossible to model with a computer, and sticks more than two fingers up at the conservation of energy. The article made clear that more research was clearly necessary. The author speculated about implausible sounding limited time dilation effects, and closed with a simple observation that whenever this radiation was detected, there was also a faint yeasty smell.

On the playing fields at Farlington I stand naked and alone. I cannot feel the cold as the briny winds assail my crevices, yet I notice how they probe and tickle my form. I am almost amused by the idea that as a normal man, if I wasn't blue already, then stood here, I soon would be. If history had followed a slightly different path, then there would already be a stadium here. As it is, these muddy pitches are stubbornly devoid of the architecture of the limited minds that imagined the unrealised future. A Brent goose flies past. It looks at me strangely, and I am sure it winks before flying away. It does not land.

I razed their Tricorn, and I built them their harbour bridge. I have ensured it never rains on match days and with a gesture I reconstituted all the old public conveniences. I think I am entitled to indulge myself. From the ground it rises, my own work, but drawing on all the designs for new stadia for inspiration – the sweeping lines of the harbour-side plans, the cascading water effect of the Tipner project, and the retail element of the Pompey Centre. Devoid of other people, and with a redundant rail link, this is my Acropolis of the anti-social. I take my seat, blocking the view of no one, and enjoy a match with non-existent players kicking a ball that exists only in my imagination. I quickly tire of this and turn the ball into reality, then run across the pitch and score a sublime goal of supreme quality. The celebration is high art, the human form in motion rendered as an exquisite, deified ballet. Well, you would wouldn't you?

On New Year's Eve 2000, Fudger's parents have a house party. After the disappointment of last year's event passing without us having to negotiate plummeting aeroplanes and the collapse of society, Fudger has surprised me by saying he would rather stay in than trawl the raucous night spots in search of romance. He has been practising his home brew techniques in recent months, and he assures me that the batch he has ready for tonight will likely see us get very messy indeed. Despite his difficult period of adjustment after life just carried on as normal last year, he has still mustered a little enthusiasm for this event, and he has even invested more cash than is sensible in a little device to help mark the occasion. In his dad's shed, he shows me his atomic clock. He doesn't know what makes it 'atomic', but he was very impressed by the advert and he seems to think I should absorb and reflect his enthusiasm in a perfectly efficient way. He gets up to go and fetch glasses from the kitchen so that we can start sampling the beer. I can see what is going to happen but cannot affect it in any way. He allows the shed door to slam, and I end up trapped in there on my own. When he stops laughing I tell him that his pressurised barrel is making a funny noise.

He tells me not to worry, and he'll try and ring his dad for advice.

Mr Packer works in a residential project and has opted for triple time rather than attend his own party. For whatever reason, no one at the project answers the phone. A couple of hours later no one is laughing any more, and I am trying to make Fudger understand that the noises from the volatile container that I find myself in close proximity to are making me very nervous. Opening a drawer in the old desk that serves as a work bench, I find a stack of old programmes to look at. I am still stuck in the shed as midnight approaches. All the party goers are indoors, except Fudger who is peering in the window and trying to make me feel better. I stare at his atomic clock and see the last few seconds of the millennium tick away. The yeasty smell becomes unbearable in the back of my head, and as the zeroes all align in the display, my mind is awash with an indescribable sense of starlight and thumbnail moons of every size whizzing in all directions. Barely a few metres away, a broken carriage clock is stopped at twelve o'clock. In an immeasurable nothing of a second I cease to be. The explosion registers no sound in my ears. I am not there, yet I can see Fudger blown onto his backside. There are lawnmower parts and charred pages of football programmes all about him, a stupid look on his face, and a mess in his trousers.

A couple of weeks later, in the garden of their house near the station, I put myself slowly back together. I am not as I once was. Some changes have been wrought upon me, I have no hair or clothes. Turning blue was my idea. In no time, I am invited across the railway line and into the mainstream consciousness of the fans, and the city beyond. They want me to wear a sailor suit, but I decline, condescending only to wear their symbol on my forehead.

The club's fortunes will continue to go in cycles. It will not last forever, yet there will be very interesting times in the years to come.

When they interview me for the New Scientist, I reveal my continuing research into the confounding energy particles that have become known as 'frattons'. They hint at unbelievably exciting possibilities and futures. Even I do not yet fully understand their properties, nor whether their associated time effects mean that they caused the explosion, or were derived from it. I am able to fashion insights into all timelines save my own, yet I feel I can confidently claim that this accident, or pre-destined metamorphosis, has presented me with the ability to view things differently, things of the now, the yesterday and the yet to come. I hope to be worthy of the gift.

## No Tactical Voting, Labour Can Win Portsmouth

## Claire Udy (2017)

I was hidden in my room, laptop open and Twitter was alight with talk of Theresa May calling an emergency press conference.

'That's it,' I initially thought, 'nuclear war is on its way.'

In a moment of pure melodrama, I was frantically messaging my working husband setting out our end of the world plan. Instead, 11 a.m. arrived and the sinking feeling didn't disappear as the words I feared most as a Labour supporter came flooding from Ms May's mouth.

General Election.

Coincidentally, we had a usual party meeting scheduled for that night, but as you can imagine everything went out the window as all of us activists had been split into two camps: fight or flight. Our meeting that night was busier than we could have ever imagined and we shared our collective grief and fear over the dreaded Lib Dem bar charts. We were not going to let tactical voting take the wind from our sails.

When I *finally* got round to voting in my first General Election in 2010 (I turned 18 in 2006) as a lifelong resident of Portsmouth South, Mike Hancock was the glaringly obvious choice. I did not want a Conservative winning in my constituency, and I thought I was doing my bit to help him keep his seat, being a, dare I say it, patriot for Portsmouth. I've always considered myself to be a socialist and at this stage I was still angry at Labour for the Iraq War (I had tippexed 'No War' on my backpack in senior school and refused to go to lessons).

I was also considering going to university as a mature student, and as free tuition was a policy pledge, the Lib Dems had me. What I didn't expect was the Lib Dems entering a coalition with the Conservatives. *And then* they went back on the tuition fee pledge. I am still rather bitter about that, amongst other things the Lib Dems have done whilst having control of the council locally. I am not the only one.

I finally joined Labour on the wave of Jeremy Corbyn becoming leader in late 2015 (and if you are a student thinking of a joining, do it, it's £1 a year). I dragged myself to a Southsea branch meeting one cold night in January where there were lots of people. What I remember most vividly was the older women drinking Guinness (that's my drink too!) and I realised that I had found my spiritual home. I'm still annoyed about Iraq, but the new members and returning ones found solidarity in the fact that Tony Blair was a let-down despite producing the best elections results for Labour in decades. That and we fucking hated the Tories. Anyway, back to the matter at hand: the General Election.

This past week, a huge group of us have worked to deliver 42,000 leaflets in Portsmouth South, all bearing the face (and beautifully moody photos) of your local Labour candidate, Stephen Morgan. Stephen was born in Portsmouth, educated in local state schools and lives in the city. His campaign to become a councillor in Charles Dickens ward saw him unseat Lib Dem Margaret Foster after a twelve-year reign. He has also become my mentor and is an incredibly hard-working person who literally never stops. He was finally selected by the party on the 2nd of May, but by this point the Lib Dems had already stolen the march with one of their classic leaflets replete with dodgy bar chart!

*Groan.*

This is the first thing the electorate here in Portsmouth South had seen, and it certainly has tongues wagging. What the Lib Dems fail to mention is that their vote collapsed in 2015 due to a mixture of propping up a Conservative government, going back on their tuition fee pledge, and having their ex-MP of over twenty years embroiled in a row over claims he had sexually assaulted a vulnerable constituent. The local Lib Dems had also made over £1.2 million of cuts to Sure Start Centres in 2013, a trend which was continued by the Conservative council three years later.

What I am trying to say is that the Lib Dems have failed Portsmouth, but they don't want you to remember that.

How do they make you forget? By telling you that Labour can't win here.

It scares the electorate into a tactical vote because the only thing we do have in common (or at least I think we do) is that we don't want the Conservatives in government. When leafleting this week, I had my fair share of residents bound out of the front doors of their houses all excited that Labour had finally got a leaflet out but they also wanted to tell me that they were thinking of voting tactically.

'Hey! Labour will just split the anti-tory vote and Flick will get back in!'

Ahhhh, no. You're assuming people will be voting for Liberal Democrats in droves, but this is in no way the case. In 2015, the Liberal Democrats lost a considerable share of their vote (see above). Both Labour and the Tories capitalised on this fall and it has put Labour in a 'fair game' bracket with the Lib Dems to contest the seat. Labour are working hard, and with 800 members in Portsmouth South alone, we have been able to mobilise a grass roots campaign to get in touch with the electorate.

'Why are you contesting a seat you've never won?'

Remember in 2014 in the local elections when UKIP stormed the country and even got five seats on Portsmouth City Council? They didn't even have to get off the sofa to win that one. The idea that a party can't win a seat simply because they haven't done before is a laughable notion and a pretty negative way to view the world. Who wants to be told they are not capable of change? That things will always be the same no matter how hard you try? Portsmouth Labour are proud to say we almost have a member in every street in Portsmouth South. Imagine the visibility if they all just put a poster in their window at the very least?

'Why don't you just stand aside?'

Stephen Morgan has been a breath of fresh air in the council, and he is paving the way for a younger generation of aspiring politicians who want to change the world for the better and protect public services. Why would we want to stand aside for someone who absolutely wants to make a difference?

Labour are a viable alternative to a Tory and Lib Dem government, and we would like to give the electorate the chance to vote for whom they wish. We believe our policies and our candidate have the edge over other parties and candidates here in Portsmouth and we are campaigning relentlessly to get Stephen elected.

We are living in a world where extraordinary things happen every day. Many have claimed we are living in a simulation, whilst others have read up on Billionaire Robert Mercer and the role of Cambridge Analytica in politics on both sides of the Atlantic. Trump was elected, Britain voted to leave the EU and almost as astonishingly, our Eurovision entry did not get the dreaded 'nil points' as expected.

Labour winning may well be considered extraordinary but it is more than achievable. Literally all you have to do is vote.

Do I want the Tories out? Absolutely! Do we live in a society where as a democracy we can choose who we vote for? Yes! Do I want to restrict that choice? Hell no! We may not have proportional representation but we still have the right to exercise our vote. If you want to vote Labour in this election, don't give in to the fear, put an x in that box! Also, seeing UKIP lose their deposit would be a glorious bonus, so let us do that too.

PS I'm hedging my bets on a grassroots movement winning this to the point that if it does then I will get the word "grARSEroots" tattooed on my butt.

## Penny Mordaunt's Turkish Tall Story

### Richard Williams (2017)

It took me less than a minute. A quick search on Google to find the European Commission website on EU Enlargement.

Despite the EU's (often justified) reputation for obtuseness and over-complexity, the language used is clear. Every current EU member state has a veto on the accession of any new EU member. Not only this, but they have a veto on the negotiation of every one of the 35 policy areas that the country looking to join has to progress through before the final accession treaty can be put to each member state.

The following is lifted directly from the EU website:

*'Concluding the negotiations*

*1. Closing the chapters ('chapters' are policy areas, of which there are 35 in total)*

*No negotiations on any individual chapter are closed until every EU government is satisfied with the candidate's progress in that policy field, as analysed by the Commission.*

*And the whole negotiation process is only concluded definitively once every chapter has been closed.*

*2. Accession treaty*

*This is the document that cements the country's membership of the EU. It contains the detailed terms and conditions of membership, all transitional arrangements and deadlines, as well as details of financial arrangements and any safeguard clauses.*

*It is not final and binding until it:*
- *wins the support of the EU Council, the Commission, and the European Parliament*
- *is signed by the candidate country and representatives of all existing EU countries*
- *is ratified by the candidate country and every individual EU country, according to their constitutional rules (parliamentary vote, referendum, etc.).'*

So, if I could find this information so easily, why couldn't my MP, Penny Mordaunt, do the same before making her claim last year that Turkey was about to join the EU, and there was nothing Britain could do about it?

Her claim was picked up by the mainstream press. On the same day the *Daily Express* (who perhaps unsurprisingly also failed to check for the truth) led with '"Turkish Migrants to CRIPPLE the NHS" Brexit minister's stark WARNING.'

The *Daily Mail* ran with the following: 'Penny Mordaunt said it is "very likely" Turkey will join the EU within the next eight years and claimed Britain doesn't have a veto to stop it joining. This would make the UK vulnerable to millions of terrorists, gangsters and 12 million more guns if we stay in the EU, pointing to higher murder and kidnapping rates and gun ownership in Turkey and the other four countries currently applying to join the Brussels club.'

Mordaunt was condemned by Remain politicians such as David Cameron, who implied she was lying. Others took her comments as part of a 'borderline racist' Leave campaign, and many were quick to highlight, as I have above, the facts. Highlighting the inaccuracy of Mordaunt's claim even spawned its own irreverent Twitter campaign, #MordauntFacts.

Somehow Mordaunt kept her job and the row around it soon became yesterday's news, whilst the Leave campaign continued to push the line that Turkey were joining with an inflammatory poster (see featured image, above).

However, if you read the status reports on Turkey's application (even before Erdogan's actions after the attempted coup), you will see that, of the 35 policy areas, only one (for scientific research) had been closed – all of the others are either in negotiation, or at a stage where negotiation has not even started. 8 of these areas were being held up by Turkey's refusal to accept the Ankara Protocol over Cyprus.

There are huge objections from other EU members aside from Cyprus and Greece, such as the increasingly right-wing governments of Eastern Europe, all of whom, remember, have a veto on each policy area, and any final accession. Turkey applied to join the EU (or rather the EEC at the time) in 1987, but even the most cursory glance at the documents clearly show that there is no way that Turkey is going to join the EU any time soon.

How influential was this claim by Mordaunt, in terms of Brexit? I have no idea, but I suspect it was not hugely significant. However, for me this isn't really about Brexit.

Whatever your views on the referendum result, Mordaunt made a highly contentious claim on mainstream TV, one which a couple of minutes of basic research proves to be utterly false. She has not corrected herself or apologised in any way.

As to the reasons for her original comments and subsequent lack of retraction, I guess we'll have to draw our own conclusions.

## Zapped by Emperor Galloway:
## Portsmouth UKIP, the Homeless and Science Fiction

### Justin MacCormack (2017)

In the wake of the Grenfell Tower inferno, I expected there to be a respectful pause before our politicians began calling for a purge of the poor. But no, UKIP quickly stepped up to the plate to make comments about Portsmouth's homeless population that evoked the 1973 science fiction film *Soylent Green*, which posits a gruesome solution to poverty and overpopulation.

In the wretched hive of scum and villainy – sorry, that's the Mos Eisley spaceport from *Star Wars* - what I mean is in Portsmouth City Council, in July 2017, UKIP Councillor Colin Galloway called for our police commissioner 'to put pressure on his police force to help us clean up this unwelcome detritus.'

Immediately following this statement, Mr Galloway zapped one of the nearby journalists with lightning from his fingertips – ah no, sorry, that was the evil megalomaniac emperor of the *Star Wars* films. Strange how I keep making these mistakes.

Naturally, I was curious about what kind of support – if any – Mr Galloway will offer the homeless in Portsmouth. Horrifyingly, he went on to say that the homeless 'must be removed from our city and placed in specific care whether they want to or not.' I wondered if he would be housing them in one of his spare rooms. Somehow, I doubt it.

In earnest, I asked to meet Mr Galloway and discuss his plans for caring for the most vulnerable in our society. 'You mean the poor defenceless aristocracy and their billionaire friends?" he replied. 'The homeless are like vampires. Leeches, I tell you! Quick, we must flee, before they rise from their crypts to devour us all!'

Actually, he didn't say that. Mr Galloway did not agree to meet me. I suspect that we would not get along well enough to maintain a civil conversation. After all, I was raised to believe in equality, compassion and social justice – a position which clashes sharply with a scientific study funded by UKIP and released last year which states that the poorest in society are biologically closer to newts than they are to other human beings.

OK. That didn't happen either, but it could have.

According to a Freedom of Information request made in December 2017, in 2014 126 homeless people in Portsmouth turned to the council for housing. By 2017, this had risen to 1206. These are pretty horrifying and revealing numbers. It provides some consolation that UKIP's share of the vote in the 2017 election fell by 13%.

Mr Galloway may well go on to spend the next few days trying to petition the House of Lords to pass a law allowing him to legally hunt the poor for sport, and to televise it in some kind of national *Hunger Games*-style competition. However, the rest of us can rest soundly knowing that for every crackpot UKIP councillor who says something bone-chillingly deplorable, the likes of which even a Bond villain wouldn't utter, there will be at least one other person out there offering a supporting hand to those who need it.

## Are We Losing Our Community Spirit?
## The Struggle to Keep Southsea Greenhouse Alive

### Sue Stokes (2016)

I left school with the usual teenage delusions. I thought I could fly, that my ideas had legs and that the whole world was my oyster. My thoughts had wings and my dreams ran wild. So, in a spirit of optimism I studied modern ballet at the London School of Contemporary Dance, until I crashed out a year in with an injury. At 20 years old, I very much remained a child in my mind, a significant part of my life still at home with my Mum in the kitchen and the garden, learning everything she had to teach me about living and sharing.

Roll on 35 years, and a thoroughly eventful life later (well, so far). I've had an interesting career: window dressing, regeneration in the city with The Partnership Foundation, developing children's centres, working on the children's fund – and lots more window dressing. I've been married for 30 years, I have four great kids, and some indispensable friends, I've lost a hundred pairs of specs and probably, a little of that eye for detail I had in my twenties.

But the part of my life I'd like to focus on here began in 2011, when – with a few other 'off the wall' people – I founded a Community Co-operative called 'Southsea Greenhouse'. I dreamed that Southsea Greenhouse might become a seafront flower cafe – selling flowers and crafts, serving teas and coffees, and building a community of workers, volunteers and the public.

We started small in a little painted shack on Southsea seafront. Our name came from our love of green stuff and our vision to become a place where great ideas and big dreams would grow for local artists and growers. After a while we moved to the Pyramids Centre, before settling into the community garden by Canoe Lake that we now call home.

We began trading with the loose ethos of 'loving life' and 'giving something back' – and so many people responded. Members and supporters gave thousands of working hours as they built, planted and weeded, created workshops and events, and most importantly, stopped and talked to the many garden visitors who would turn up whenever our gate was open.

As well as growing plants and veg, we grew in number; and that number moved around the city, spreading the magic. We supported other local ventures and traders, we encouraged everyone we encountered to love local and grow your own. We shared time, energy, and many cups of tea. We exchanged suppers, problems, stories and secrets – and all the joys and sadness's beneath and in between. We overcame challenges and never tired of new ideas. This boundless community became my normal for the past five years and I confess, I came to take it somewhat for granted – until its unexpected collapse prompted a huge sense of loss and grief.

I know that change happens. Sometimes you just look up and it's like everyone's gone to the moon and your invite got lost in the post. The garden that members and volunteers ran as our own Eden-inspired garden centre, with a 'pick-your-own' principle at its heart, has slowly become harder and harder to staff and manage as our volunteers began to fade away. There are fewer shoulders to share the workload and responsibility, less hands to make light work of regular tasks, and so many more things to manage and undertake with a smaller and smaller crew.

After much hand-wringing over our inability to open the garden to set, regular hours, we relaunched as a Secret Garden that opens unpredictably, in the hope that the expectations of our visitors would adapt to the limitations of what we can achieve with a smaller team of volunteers.

And still our visitors come, now with a little more curiosity and a little less tut-tutting at our irregular opening hours. They come in fits and starts, like lost sparks at a firework party.

Back in 2013, when we began our 'grow local' campaign, Southsea was ruled by supermarkets, new roads and sexy little projects that received public funding.

Now the city embraces 'wonky veg', more people are showing interest in allotments, growing veg on their balconies and in window boxes, and there are more wild blooms springing up around the city. We like to think our dreams of a garden city inspired some of this. Our own green-space in the Secret Garden is a precious thing and we want to spend our time sharing it with others, to re-discover, support and encourage some of those old handicrafts, but not to lose sight of our friends and the work that still needs to be done every day.

So, what have we learned so far?

Well, we know how it feels to hit the bottom, for a start. We're now facing the challenge of winding up our dream of a Community Co-operative, which we are now in the process of dissolving. The cooperative failed mostly because many of our old members signed up but then moved on and stopped sharing their time – a trend that appears to be echoed across the UK since the economic downturn.

The loss of so many of our volunteers saddens me. We don't live in a village, or even in a broadly benevolent community these days; we live in a city where money makes the most noise and often becomes a barrier to growth and sharing across our community. We see this in loudly voiced local opinions on refugees, and in the growing trend towards silo thinking as finding funding in an increasingly bare landscape sets local projects in competition rather than co-operation with each other, and not much is free.

There are of course exceptions – projects like Portsmouth Foodcycle, local foodbanks and campaigns like Don't Hate, Donate are great news – but they rely on the hard and unpaid labour of a small number and rely on the rest of us to help a lot more, as well as funding and practical support to survive. In a more competitive landscape where our larger and more established organisations are struggling to survive, the city's bigger players understandably gather around funding but leave in their wake smaller, independent and often grassroots community projects struggling to breathe, let alone to survive.

But I want to end on a high note, so here's a challenge for everyone. It's the kind of thing we did and still do at Southsea Greenhouse as some of Pompey's die-hard eco-warriors: sticking up for the trees and the green spaces in our city, but also for those less fortunate, for the old, the young and the lonely, who we will always welcome in our community garden at Canoe Lake.

Get involved in your local community. Read *Star & Crescent* to find groups, organisations and projects in Portsmouth by which you can do so.

One thing my lovely Mum taught me in those early, post-ballerina days back at home: make the most of those you love and always make time to share with them. If you love Pompey as much as we do, extend that spirit outwards and make ours the first city to reverse the decline in volunteering that's spreading across the country. We're in a time when building a community based on sharing is an increasingly revolutionary act, but unlike so much local and national politics, it's a revolution based on collective action rather than division.

Share what you discover with your friends in real time and in real life as well as on social media. If you can, think about ways to get involved and share some of your time and skills with your community.

It's all so much simpler – and so much more powerful – when we do it together.

## Hired Killers for the British State:
## An Interview with a Veteran for Peace

### Graham Horne (2016)

**Could you tell me about your own military experience?**

Graham Horne: I joined the army in 1973 just before my nineteenth birthday. I was a radio operator with the Royal Signals and was posted to bases in England and in West Germany where we effectively practised for when the Cold War would go hot. I never saw active service, never won any medals. The prospect of being able to do rock-climbing, abseiling, mountaineering, camping and play with radios – that was all a massive turn-on for me.

**The modern advertising campaigns present the army as a big adventure. Was it promoted like that in the 1970s?**

Yes, very much so. All these campaigns try to appeal to young people who have left school and perhaps haven't done terribly well in their exams. Telling these kids that they have nothing better to aspire to than stacking shelves or fighting a pitch battle is bad.

**When did you realise that you the army wasn't for you?**

I signed up for six years and was never a terribly good soldier. I got bored to tears doing exercises and endless menial work and just basically waiting for the Cold War to escalate. Unless you lived near the base you had to spend your weekends in this deserted wasteland where all we had was the NAAFI. The sheer boredom made me misbehave. The worst thing I did was "go over the wall" or abscond for a week. I was courting my first wife at the time so every opportunity to go home and see her was welcome. After three years' service I was entitled to buy myself out for £300. So, I did.

**I take it you didn't think much of military discipline and hierarchy?**

I've never been good at dealing with authority because of the shit education I had. Where I grew up in north Kent you left school to either work in the local paper mill or Chatham dock yard or the forces. That was it.

Has much changed since then?

The army still actively recruits children – they're only sixteen-year-olds – in economically deprived areas. We call it "economic conscription". If someone says, 'We're going to feed you, clothe you, put a roof over your head and give you ten grand a year pocket money', it's as good as conscription if the only alternative is a dead-end job or the dole.

**Tell me more about your training.**

The guys training us would talk about loyalty and self-discipline. They saw the army as one big family. In a barrack block you'll never hear talk of patriotism, queen, country or anything like that. What you will hear is talk about doing the right thing by your mates. It's a gang mentality.

What they also do in training is put a 'hierarchy of hate' in place. You're taught to feel superior to other elements of the armed forces. In the Parachute Regiment it's based on physical prowess. If you're in the Service Corps it's based on intellect. So, our attitude as radio operators was that, without our support, the Paras would just be mindless killers with no supply or communication lines. Then we were encouraged to disparage the navy. There was a lot of homophobia directed at these blokes being cooped up in ships for months on end. We used to call them the 'rum, bum and baccy boys' because we thought sailors only needed those three things to be happy.

Then we'd have vitriol towards the RAF because they had no tradition to speak of and they'd been dining out on the Battle of Britain for years. We used to call them "the crabs" because they couldn't march, they could only move sideways. Obviously, there's no truth in any of these perceptions, but this kind of hatred was encouraged.

At the bottom of the heap is the civilian population – they are moaners, whingers, couldn't hack it if they joined up. It's ironic when you think about how many civilians want to bask in the glory of the armed forces through Help for Heroes and Remembrance Sunday and so on. I can tell you that the admiration is not mutual. Our attitude was we'll get our arses shot off for civilians, but they don't deserve it. In my day this meant we had a sense of entitlement and assumed we could try it on with any passing female that took their eye.

**Are these problems still around today?**

Today a woman is twice as likely to be sexually harassed in the military as she is in another profession. It's down to the problem of an authoritarian, top-down power structure where people are afraid to complain about being treated like shit. We had horribly abusive initiation rituals when I was serving. The minute I got into the barrack block of my working unit – it was an old, condemned building with about fifteen blokes in it – I was grabbed, spread out on the table and my trousers and pants were ripped off. My genitals were covered in toothpaste and that burns badly! The next thing I did was hare off to the showers and clean myself up. But what you don't do is grass your mates. You just put up with it.

**So, it's a culture of silence that lets injustice happen?**

When it gets out of hand it can lead to the deaths at Deepcut. But in my case, when the next new bloke came through the door, I was compelled by gang loyalty to dish out the self-same abuse that I'd received.

There's also a cruel system of collective punishment. If we had a barrack room inspection and someone's bed space wasn't up to scratch the troop sergeant would say, 'Right lads, you need to deal with that otherwise you're not going anywhere this weekend and you'll be on guard duty.' We all got in trouble for a mistake made by just one guy in our unit. We had a thing called "the regimental bath" which was a tub we filled with washing up liquid, disinfectant, soap powder and our own piss. We'd grab the bloke who'd messed his bed space and throw him in it and scrub him down with a yard broom. This was to make sure he got the message that if he let himself down he'd let his whole unit down.

**Do you think the arms industry, which is closely connected to the armed forces, should be protected because it employs a lot of people?**

I'm a trades unionist and when GMB and Unite organise within the weapons industry they're not concerned about the death and destruction it causes around the world. All they can see is potential job losses. There's a passive acceptance of what President Eisenhower called the 'military-industrial complex' back in 1960. And we need a war every so often to justify the expenditure and to establish whether these hugely expensive weapons work. You can test them up to a certain point, but you'll never know how they fully perform unless they do the job for real.

**What would you say to someone working in the arms industry who doesn't agree with the harm that industry does, but also doesn't want to end up unemployed?**

It's a tough call. Back in the 1970s, a company called Lucas gave up defence work and moved into eco-friendly manufacturing. Other companies ought to diversify into peacetime pursuits.

Does your organisation Veterans for Peace oppose all violence under any circumstance?

If someone attacked my family I wouldn't be answerable for what I did. As an organisation we've come to the conclusion that war is usually a failure of foreign policy. Both world wars could have been avoided through peaceful means, for example. War protects the privileges of ruling elites and the only people who get anything out of it are those who don't have to do the dirty work. When working class soldiers were demobbed after the world wars they were supposed to be going back to "a land fit for heroes". That demonstrably wasn't true. In most cases they went back to poverty and unemployment.

**Would you say that's true of servicemen and women returning from more recent conflicts?**

There's sod all for them. VfP has real problems with Help for Heroes because it buys into militarism, sentimentality and hero worship. We in VfP don't see ourselves as heroes – we were hired killers for the British state. We were given guns, told to go and kill people and then, when it was no longer convenient, we were told, 'F*** off, we don't need you anymore.'

Help for Heroes never question the basis of a war like Iraq which, as we all know, was highly illegal under international law. They don't understand that the veterans they try and help were injured for no good reason in wars of aggression that killed hundreds of thousands of innocent civilians. I don't see that as heroic.

**Do you feel you personally were poorly treated when you came out of the army?**

I once lost my temper at the Job Centre, jumped out of my chair and shouted at the clerk, 'Look you bastard, if it wasn't for me you'd be speaking Russian.' I was physically escorted out of the building.

## All of Me

### Helen Larham (2017)

I have always loved him
despite his neglect
so when I stepped out onto the sea
he bore my full weight, everything:
All those times I had ventured in
and they had laughed
at my frantic back stroking
and butterflying like a frog.
My woollen costume
expanding in the water
corrugating, like elephant skin
uncovering yards of goose flesh.
He took all of me.

The sea laid himself flat, calm.
Cradled me, gently nudging
until I obliged and turned on my back.
Floating weightless, untethered
drifting away from myself.
He let me have all of him;
Sometimes with waves as high
as my neck could crane
swirling me up in a whirlpool
then down to the ghost wrecks below.
Other times rocking me asleep
in the grey mist.

When he at last grew tired of our games
he beached me at my home port
gave me back to the land-
to my family.
I sat silent till the lights blossomed
in the black, just beyond the threshold
of the town.
I sat with the whole expanse of him
still echoing in my head
and with the tidal moon
still lapping at my blood.

## Somerstown's Reputation Hides a Surprising Reality

### Kelly Turner (2017)

Somerstown began life as a working-class residential district in the early nineteenth century. In the 1950s, Somers Road was lined with shops and a school, which gave it the feel of a village. By 1964, the district consisted of tiny Victorian so-called 'houses for artisans'. In the mid to late-1960s houses on the western side of Somers Road were demolished to make way for 'high rise, medium rise flats and a modicum of two-storey houses.' Some 1,245 new dwellings were built inside an area of 33 acres. Judged by today's standards these were modern slums.

I live in Somers Road in an ugly five-storey block with no attractive features. The even higher blocks adjacent to me are equally foreboding. The old saying goes 'beauty is only skin deep': while Somerstown may be ugly, there is beauty on the inside.

I didn't know this as I was preparing to move there. A quick Google search revealed that I had apparently chosen to live in one of the most horrible, dangerous areas of Portsmouth. Phrases like 'soul destroying', 'deprived', 'bit risky', 'your car will get vandalised' popped out and, hard as I tried, I could scarcely find any positive reviews.

I was worried I'd made a serious mistake.

However, time has shown me that the serious mistake I made was to judge the area on appearances and misinformed prejudices. My neighbours come from a diverse mix of ethnic and social backgrounds, and they're all pleasant and friendly.

So why the bad press? Police statistics for the St Thomas ward – which encompasses Somerstown – show that most of the crimes occurring in the area relate to antisocial behaviour (ASB). From January to April 2017, 435 such offences were recorded. During the same period there were 189 violent and sexual crimes.

I asked the Police Team leader for our area, Inspector Marcus Cator if crime in Somerstown is higher than it was ten years ago. He pointed out that extensive shifts in the ways in which crime is recorded, together with other social and technological developments mean that comparing past and present statistics cannot easily show whether crime has gone up or down.

'The style of crime has changed as the means by which to commit it has forced change,' he said. 'Cars cannot be broken into like they used to. Cars cannot be stolen like they used to. Houses and windows are more secure. So, crime types in certain areas have changed massively through problem solving, crime prevention and manufacture changes over ten years.

'People have more communication facilities so they tell us more as and when these crimes happen,' he said. 'The calls for service to police and partners have risen massively and the expectations for service have risen with it.'

I asked Inspector Cator if he felt Somerstown was a dangerous area.

'No, not in comparison to the rest of Portsmouth,' he said.

The statistics highlight two areas in the city that have higher problems with anti-social behaviour. There were 417 ASB offences reported in St Thomas ward from January to April 2017, and over the same period, 981 ASB offences were reported in Charles Dickens, and 430 in Nelson ward.

I have spoken to a range of people about their views of Somerstown and Portsmouth as a whole. One elderly gentleman told me that a former boss told him to always say he lived in Southsea, never Portsmouth. He also said that, thirty years ago, if you were to tell an employer you lived in Leigh Park (another large council estate in Havant, just outside Portsmouth) you would not get a job. I then told him I lived in Somerstown. Apparently back then I would have struggled to get a job as well. It seems these council estates have always been viewed negatively, with words such as 'common' and 'scum' being thrown around, even from one of the nicest elderly gentlemen I have met.

A German national, resident in Portsmouth, was horrified to find out where I live. She too had only heard negative things about the area. How dangerous it is, how to never walk alone there at night and so on. But she had never actually seen Somerstown for herself and was apparently unaware of the relatively low crime rate here. I invited her to my flat so she could see what the area was like. She politely declined my offer.

Many of these skewed opinions stem from people who have only walked through the area or heard about it, but not actually lived here. I decided to speak to some of the residents of Somerstown. From these small conversations it became apparent to me that Somerstownians are happy with where they live and they don't view it as dangerous.

They agreed that other residents are friendly, however, the majority shared the opinion that Somerstown looks horrible. The buildings were described to me as 'ugly', 'old' and 'un-homely'.

If you walk through Somerstown, don't worry about being attacked. Just avoid looking too harshly at the eye-sores, you don't want to damage your eyes.

# If Portsmouth Housing Associations Can't Provide 'Affordable' Housing, Who Can?

## Cal Corkery (2018)

On 14 February 2018, Southern Housing Group, a major national housing association, were advertising four one-bedroom flats in Portsmouth on Rightmove. The rent on these properties ranged from £460pcm (per calendar month) to £670pcm, described as an 'affordable rent'.

'Affordable rent' refers to rents charged at 80% of the market rate, and were introduced by the government in 2010. The policy allows landlords to offer less secure tenancies than are available to social housing tenants. The problem is, homelessness charity Shelter reports, that 'rents in social rented homes ... are typically about 50% of market rents, with life-long tenancies. So social rented homes are – for low income families – much more affordable than Affordable Rent and much more secure.'

Clause 150 of the Localism Act 2011 compels every local housing authority in the UK to publish a tenancy strategy, which all local providers of social housing must observe. Section VI of Portsmouth City Council's Tenancy Strategy states that providers must ensure 'Homes remain affordable and do not exceed Local Housing Allowance (LHA) levels'.

The LHA rate in each area is used to work out how much housing benefit is received by tenants in homes provided by a private landlord. The LHA for a one-bedroom property in Portsmouth is £504.57 pcm.

Three of the four local properties advertised on Rightmove by Southern Housing Group exceed the LHA and, as such, fail to comply with the Portsmouth Tenancy Strategy. The most expensive property is £165.43 pcm more than the LHA rate.

But perhaps even more significant is why these properties are being advertised on Rightmove by a housing association at all. Wouldn't we expect all housing association properties to be allocated by the council to those in most need? After all, this is what happens with almost all other social and (genuinely) affordable rent stock in Portsmouth.

The Rightmove adverts state that, to apply for any of these properties, the prospective tenant must be in employment and earning above a certain salary threshold. The £670 flat in Portsea is only available to those earning at least £20,099 which equates to over £10 an hour (see image below).

While providing housing at sub-market rents to people in work is an admirable and necessary objective, there is currently a major shortage of local social housing supply. It is concerning that not all housing association properties are being let to those in most housing need.

By 27 February, 3 of the 4 one-bedroom properties previously listed were still vacant. Perhaps they still are – you can find out by looking on their website. Meanwhile, there are local single people and couples sleeping rough in temperatures below zero as blizzards sweep the country.

I first contacted Portsmouth City Council about this issue in December 2017. I am still awaiting a substantive response. I'll let you know if ever I receive one.

## Portsmouth City Council Must Support Homeless People, Not Scapegoat Them

### Alan Burgess (2017)

*'Portsmouth City is no longer a welcoming city to either business or tourist because it seems we prefer to have vagrants. It is time to get our Police and Crime Commissioner to put pressure on his police force to help us clean up this unwelcome detritus. These beggars, vagrants, rough sleepers, homeless, troubled folks or whatever label you want to put on them must be removed from our city and placed in specific care whether they want to or not. We have tried the soft approach and have found it wanting. It's time for some serious tough love. We need to save our city and we need to save these lost souls. This Chamber asks the Leader of the Council to write to the Police and Crime Commissioner to instruct the local police force to be more vigilant and to help the Council to remove the ever-increasing beggars and rough sleepers that are beginning to dominate the city.'*
- Cllr Colin Galloway (UKIP), Notice of a Motion on 'Homelessness', meeting of Full Council, Portsmouth 11 July 2017.

In his recent motion (see above for excerpt) Cllr Colin Galloway not only uses the term 'unwelcome detritus' to describe human beings, but also - following widespread outrage and criticism in response to the motion – emphasised to the BBC that his words 'had done the job.'

What seems to be beyond the grasp of Cllr Galloway is the risk his inflammatory language is adding to an already problematic situation. Currently a homeless man or woman is at risk of violence, with a case earlier this year of a Portsmouth homeless man's possessions being urinated on and set on fire. Describing homeless people as 'detritus' publicly, in the press, will increase this risk. This language is wholly unacceptable, and many – myself among them -   called on Cllr Galloway to resign.

Cllr Galloway does not stop at offensive language directed at the vulnerable. He calls on the police to 'remove' beggars and rough sleepers. As others have pointed out, this sounds like internment, and is likely to create more problems than it will solve. The Council's Homeless Working Group report – a working group that includes Cllr Galloway – includes a section on enforcement. It is very clear that the police have no powers to round up rough sleepers, and even if they had, what would the police do with 60 or more people to care for? Already the police complain that mental health sufferers from the wider community are landing in their cells due to a lack of adequate provision.

Interestingly, Superintendent Will Schofield pointed out to the Homeless Working Group that, according to the law, the police must direct rough sleepers to accommodation. Presumably this would mean police escorting rough sleepers to the counter of Housing Options at the Civic?

And what exactly are the options at Housing Options? Section 5.3 of the Homeless Working Group report states: 'The number of supported bed spaces in the City is 205, of which 160 is [sic] for single people. During the past year there have been 387 referrals for supported housing from single people.'

In other words, demand outstrips capacity by 242%. This, of course, may be why people sleep rough: there is insufficient capacity provided by public services.

This crisis in public provision has a context. Cuts to local government budgets from central government, a sharp decline in the availability of social housing and a sharp increase in rent for private accommodation. Portsmouth City Council cannot passively stand by and watch while the combination of these forces crush the most vulnerable in our community.

As a proud member of PACT, Portsmouth Against the Cuts Together, I can say confidently that the Council were warned of the impact of cuts and council worker redundancy back in 2012. The Council's budget papers for 2017/18 stated, 'Over the past 6 years (since 2011/12), Central Government funding to Portsmouth City Council has reduced by over £68m (amounting a 44% cut in total Government Funding).'

However, I must stress to the council that it is comprehensively failing in its duty by failing to support those most in need in our community. The Council urgently need sufficient resources to house rough sleepers, not scapegoat them.

The leader of the council Donna Jones commented in the Portsmouth News on 5th January 2017, 'This isn't about housing or money, this is about supporting people's mental health needs.'

When I read this, I thought I had fallen down a rabbit hole. On what planet does the leader of the council reside? Is it a planet where the homeless – i.e. people without a home – do not have a housing need? If this is the leadership of the council, it is a leadership that needs to be robustly challenged.

I would like to finish by commending the work of the Homeless Working Group and the supporting workers of the council. I would like to stress that this work is urgent and needs the fastest response possible.

There are many in our community that are watching the development of this issue as it unfolds. We ask the council to look closely at this matter and provide progressive and humane responses as soon as possible.

## A Brief Walk Around God, Ignorance and Southsea

### Sudip Sen (2015)

I am trying to find that in-between space, somewhere between Richard Dawkins and Isis; between Page 3 and the niqab. But all the while, I am humming that 'Take Me to Church' song by Hozier: 'I'll worship like a dog at the shrine of your lies...' So, for those of you who know it, you will understand that I am closer to the Dawkins end of that particular spectrum.     It was a bright winter Saturday in Southsea, with no cloud to take the edges off the chill. Heading into Fratton, I walked past the entrance to the Jami Mosque and was struck by the sign with the arrow on it, a version of the symbol for the return key on my computer keyboard, which directs the faithful women to their separate entrance at the rear.

I dislike the separation of men and women in this way. I especially dislike the separation of our children into any school where faith determines who may or may not enter, and where teachers within it separate the genders for anything other than educational reasons. And anyway, Sunday school is for Sundays. I am fully aware how uninterested the faithful may be in my reaction to the sign, but it's helpful to declare this up front, I think.

I looked into it a little and found myself in some nasty company: people who would not hesitate to take one look at my brown skin and decide that I was part of a series of problems in their imagination. In the news, one can't object to a faith school without leaving a pig's head spiked on a stick it seems. And express doubts about the Divine, and you may then be a part of a smear campaign. This is loaded territory.

Is there a space to write safely about these things? I also discovered proud women saying they didn't want to be praying in front of the men anyway, with their bums in the air. But there is a bigotry there too, isn't there? Apparently, even with the most modest clothing imaginable, the devout men in the mosque simply could not help themselves and their notorious thoughts.

What does this version of faith say about men? It has always bothered me that the responsibility to remain modest falls entirely on the women. If I were a teenage girl, I may well be tempted to cover my flesh and contours as a matter of choice, but that would only be because I have gotten to know what is actually in the heads of some of the adolescent boys around me. But Sharia law is not the answer either. We need a cultural shift (banning page 3 would help, but freeing the nipple might not). We need to educate boys and girls to avoid an over-emphasis on appearance, and to nurture and protect the default position that they are equals. I accept that there is no stopping raging hormones and the second glances of our animal instincts, but if my son learns that a good brain is a very sexy thing relatively early on, then I think life will be more interesting for him.

I asked my friend's other half how she feels about it (yes, some of my best friends are Muslim). She doesn't like such signs either and her deep frustration stems from both her deep understanding of and dedication to her faith. She told me that her grandfather actually never favoured boys over girls, and her father never prevented her from competing in races at school, and her husband has no rules for her at all. For her, and for campaigning Muslim women who want a better mosque experience, there is no justification within the faith for dividing men and women in quite this way. The frustration is much greater for the faithful and progressive than it is for those such as myself who are interested but agnostic.

Again, I do not find it pleasant to walk past the sign. But in the end, I know it is allowed: it is an exemption to the Equality Act. A person who thinks like me must tolerate these religious exemptions for the moment, while we wait for the progressive forces within the churches and mosques to catch up to a more reasonable understanding of men and women, and sex and sexuality. But I can respect the faithful exactly up to the point where they tick over into a sort of prejudice, usually against gays and lesbians, or based on 'natural' roles for men and women. When one encounters those views, I think one is obliged not to let them slide without challenge. And I do not believe the defensive faithful for a second when they say that they are not judging anyone. That protest itself is a judgment.

If you want to understand a person, do not listen to what they say they believe, but watch – if you can – how they behave, especially in the company of those who they think agree with them. It is in those spaces where prejudices emerge. And remember, God is watching them watching porn on the computer anyway, so God can sort that out in due course.

Later that Saturday night, I walked along Elm Grove on the way back from Albert Road, less worse for wear than many a student around me. Three giant lads were laddishly stumbling toward me. I expect they will be chaps when they get older. They were not from the area, in shirts selected from the pink palette and sweaters tied around their waists. They were a long way from Fulham, I thought. Were they from Chichester? Were they named Tarquin? They saw me and one of them, feeling jolly as one does with a few drinks inside of one, gave me the full 'Allah-o-Akbar' [sic], both arms raised to the sky, chuckling. To quote him directly, he said, 'Oh, here's one of the Allah-o-Akbars now'. (I didn't even have a beard or anything at the time.) Another giant lad shushed him, embarrassed not by the content of his friend's behaviour, but the visibility of it. 'Not in public,' he hissed, 'not in public.'

I was then going to write that perhaps it was one of you having a good night out on the sauce. But I have learned over the years that the people who read *Star & Crescent* and the pink-shirted lads tend not to overlap. That's a sad state of affairs, but the subject of another piece entirely. I do flick through the Telegraph and Sun editorials occasionally, to get in touch, with what the Great British Public are being told they think. I recommend it to everyone, but I digress.

On the Sunday morning, as I was walking through Southsea Common, a friendly doddery old gentleman, who for no sinister reason had been giving my son biscuits on the way to school for well over a year, gave me a wave from a near distance, but also a friendly 'Salaam Walekum' (don't ask me what that is, but he was doing his best). There was no hint of a snarl at the edges of his greeting, nor a longing for the Southsea he used to know. Knowing him quite well, it was easy to conclude that he was just being friendly. I was with my brown friend and his son too. This must have distracted him, as he did not seem to recognise me at all. But I gave him a wave and a 'Good morning' back.

Later, hovering at one of the market stalls on Palmerston Road selling the over-priced olives, I heard a middle-aged white male explaining to his mother how he had recently 'discovered' the 'Arab shop' on Palmerston Road. By this, he meant a shop called Akram's Spice Cave (aka 'The Aladdin's Cave' which appears to have won a local campaign). No-one who works there could be described as coming from the Middle East. He then went on about his trip to Egypt, which was also full of Arabs, no doubt, and olives.

Let me be clear, it is not ignorance per se that bothers me – we all have holes in what we know about. I am reminded of that every day. It is ignorance with conviction: ignorance that comes from a lifetime of not being minimally interested enough in the world to learn the difference between Bangladeshis and those from the Middle East; the ignorance of assuming that a brown person must be a Muslim. This affects some of us more than others.

There were times in the past (maybe three times in the last twelve years), when particular people felt the need to indicate to me that I was a Muslim and not particularly welcome, when I would have replied with a 'Guten morgen' or a 'Guten tag' and then pretended to have confused said white person with a German. I must confess this was generally directed at the older generation who were most offended at the prospect of being mistaken for German.  In one of the less friendly conversations this prompted, I followed up with a query about why England persists with a German royal family. I do know this is unkind, but I am only human. And that old neighbour can be extremely rude.

So anyway, these few local encounters got me thinking. There I was, pondering the women's-entrance-at-the-rear sign and the exemptions to the Equality Act, and how long they might take to die off, as I hope they will, but also walking past these people, young and old, to whom I was automatically a Muslim. It is my habit to pick on blind spots as I see them. You may well wish to point out my own. But to me, there is a blind spot in a wide-eyed celebration of all of diversity even if it means that women are in a separate room in a mosque, where the men are legally entitled to keep them, for the moment. And there are also the more obvious blind spots, where I am greeted or treated as one of those men.

## Bramble

## Margaret Jennings (2016)

*(Blackberry brambles can be stripped of their thorns and used to fashion baskets and other useful artefacts).*

The first man clips off her thorns one by one,
turns her placid and tractable,
cuts her off close to the roots,
twists her into something useful,
something of his own making.

The second man threads her through a hole
in a tin which tears off her thorns,
shreds her pristine flesh.
This task makes a sound like a strimmer,
reshaping, remoulding, destroying.
He puts string in her carcass.

The last man leaves the thorns that defend her,
allows her blossom to feed the bees nectar
and helps her grow the fruit
that might bloody his fingers,
applauds as she strives for the tops of trees,
rejoices as she waves at the sun,
becoming all she was meant to become.

## Teaching, a Profession in Crisis

### Suzy Horton (2017)

One of the things that unites us is our belief that education and learning are good things. Even politicians of all parties are usually on the same page in aspiring to create the 'best' schools for our children.

I was lucky enough to speak at a national conference a few weeks ago about teacher recruitment and retention. With applications for teacher training down by 10% nationally and nearly a third of teachers leaving the profession within 5 years, teaching is at crisis point.

I was one of those children who lined up teddy bears and dolls whilst parading in front of them taking a register. Apart from a brief spell of wanting to be a zoo keeper, I never wanted to be anything other than a teacher.

I don't know exactly why. Where does that vocational drive come from? Perhaps it's a personality thing. Perhaps it was role models from my own schooling (Mrs Ide-Smith, Mr Downes, Mrs Bryant or Mr Clayton all spring to mind). Or reading stories like Enid Blyton's *Malory Towers* and *St Clares*.

What I do know is that wanting to be a teacher came more from a desire to help, nurture and enable others than a desire to earn a certain salary, have long holidays or analyse lots of data.

The profession I went into was much as I hoped and dreamed it would be. When I left, 14 years later, it was already severely compromised, however it is an altogether different career today.

I started teaching in 1989, just after the 1988 Education Reform Act which began almost three decades of changes that have led us to where we are today. The Act also fired the starting gun that:

- Promotes a narrow and prescribed curriculum
- Limits the content and breadth of what is learned
- Reduces learning to lists of skills and knowledge
- Measures and quantifies everything
- Reduces the autonomy of teachers
- Creates an evidence-based culture
- Stifles spontaneity and creativity

- Increases workload
- Introduces one new initiative after another
- Introduced league tables which pitch school against school

Unforgivably, the impact of the 1988 Act also makes success competitive instead of creating success for all. And all the while, still teachers focus on relationships as the most important ingredient in learning.

This is what the marketisation of education and micro-management of learning looks like: where data, growth and measurements trump experiences, relationships and enjoyment. It took us nearly 30 years to get to this situation and now is the time to begin the movement to save the profession. I left teaching half way along that journey, with the utmost admiration for colleagues who stayed despite an effective pay cut, worsening working conditions due to funding changes and increased workloads.

So how do we start to change things for the better?

First, we need to value the profession. The days of automatic respect for teachers have long gone but most people can appreciate that the woes of society, and the behaviour and actions of children cannot be the sole responsibility of teachers. We need to thank and admire teachers, rather than attack and blame them.

We then need to rebuild morale and re-instigate a sense of belonging in a profession that is fragmented and divided.

I honestly don't think classroom teachers enter the profession for the money; but year on year effective pay cuts are no way to reward and inspire teachers (I appreciate this is the case for most other public and many private sector workers too). We need to give them back their lost salaries by lifting the 1% pay cap.

We need to address working conditions: by reducing bureaucracy (how many data spreadsheets are genuinely used beyond demonstrating compliance with an enforced method of accountability?), by reversing the cut-to-the-bone damage inflicted by the latest funding cuts (which lead teachers to buy classroom supplies themselves), and by dealing with classroom support cuts.

But most of all, we need to again make relationships the focus of teaching and learning; with permission and encouragement from OFSTED and from school leaders and managers. We need to give teachers the freedom, choice and space to instil lifelong learning, way beyond the league tables.

I was lucky to enjoy such a job for the first few years of my teaching career – no imposed schemes of work, no SATS, no monitoring, no OFSTED, no data crunching, no performance management.

Did I work hard? Yes.

Was I totally exhausted at the end of 10-, 12- and sometimes 14-hour days? You bet.

Did I work big chunks of my holidays? Of course.

But every bit of that energy and effort went to making, creating and preparing the things that I felt the children in my class needed next. Never have I worked so hard in a job, but never have I done a job where I felt so fulfilled.

I'm convinced that there must still be children in front of a line of teddies with a desire to help, nurture and enable others. I hope that things change in education so that those children become teachers and stay in the profession for their whole career.

# I Was Attacked for Being Disabled

## Paige Tabone (2016)

Many scenarios go through your head before a night out. You imagine stumbling around singing with your friends or regretting the kebab that seemed like a good idea at the time. What you never imagine, though, is getting violently assaulted. A night in November 2014 ended just that way for me; and all because I was in a wheelchair.

Last year, *The Independent* reported on a Freedom of Information request that revealed 'hate crimes recorded by police [rose] to 2,765 incidents in 2014-15 compared to 1,955 incidents in 2013-14' – an increase of 41% in just one year. Since it was first made a criminal offence in 2007, prosecutions for disability related hate crimes have risen by an unbelievable 213% in Great Britain alone.

But does our justice system serve the victims? It didn't for me.

My injuries included bruising, scratches and scarring. I needed months of counselling to deal with the emotional damage I incurred. But, despite the police arriving immediately at the crime scene, my attacker was set free the same night with a £50 fine. I was told there wasn't sufficient evidence to prove I was targeted purely due to my disability.

But months after the incident, the officer who'd arrived at the original crime scene candidly told me that if I'd been a person of colour my assailant would have faced a far worse punishment than a fine. Why? What is it that makes one form of hate offence more or less unjust than another?

Statistics UK reports that nearly 68% of all race- or religion-oriented crimes are escalated to court proceedings compared with only 32% of disability related offences.

Lord Ken MacDonald, the former Director of Public Prosecutions, believes this anomaly is down to a lack of knowledge amongst police. He told me, 'We don't seem to have latched on to the fact yet that this has happened to them simply because they're disabled. They [the police] are looking for a deeper meaning in the attack, than just simply prosecuting them for discrimination ... it's down to a simple training fault.'

According to the Metropolitan Police Service's online training guide, officers must serve a two-year probation period during which they complete the Initial Police Learning and Development Programme (IPLDP). They learn about public protection and basic crime prevention (which has a sub-section for hate crime). However, up until 2010, there was no mention of disability hate crime in the core training and with no follow-up training required, it is easy to see how the police are not properly equipped to deal with this new type of misdemeanour.

Hate crime is not just physical. Online emotional abuse is now just as often reported to police as bodily harm. Calum Faulkner is an 18-year-old student from Berkshire who suffers from Duchenne Muscular Dystrophy. Last year, he went to the police after falling foul of online hate. 'I started to receive horrible and personal messages over social media sites, they'd say things like "go f*** yourself cripple".'

Calum tried to ignore the messages but they kept coming. After several months of suffering in silence he acted.

'I went straight down to my local police station with printed copies of the messages and without investigation they simply told me to contact the website to get it sorted, and that there was nothing they could do for me.'

As the messages contained no threats of physical violence, the police dismissed his case. He argues that he suffered as much from this 'virtual' violence as he would have done from physical abuse. 'I couldn't leave the house for weeks. I refused to go into college because I was convinced that the people sending the messages would be there.' He added, 'I might [as] well have just been hit – at least then people could see the hurt that had been caused.'

It's not just the police who are confused about the seriousness of disability hate crime. Society must understand at what point a few nasty words or an altercation becomes something graver.

I surveyed the public to find out what they really know about hate crime. I was shocked by some of the results. Nearly a quarter of the respondents believed that a hate crime exclusively involved racist or homophobic language. 23% believed that only an act of physical violence could be defined as a hate crime. Only 6% mentioned that offences against disabled people could count as hate crimes. Most troublingly to me, though, a clear majority didn't even know hate crime existed as a separate category under the law.

To me that's the problem: most of us are so ill-informed about the law that we simply don't know what is wrong with it. And too little is being done to combat the crisis. I contacted several MPs and numerous government officials to discuss this. All declined to comment.

We urgently need change because the number of victims is ever-growing. The Disability Hate Crime Network, a volunteer-based organisation, surveyed the UK's disabled community and found that 57% of respondents had suffered an attack on the street. One fifth had received abuse on public transport and a quarter had experienced incidents at home. Many said they had been the victims of cruelty and bullying on social media, just like Calum.

If we carry on in this direction we may devolve into a society of prehistoric brutes grunting about our dislike for people with slightly big ears. I'd rather we all calmed down and took a deep breath; humanity has enough battles to face, without us fighting – and hating – amongst ourselves.

## Springtime in Chernobyl

## David Angus (2016)

Why Chernobyl? Good question. I'd gone to Kiev for a science fiction convention and Chernobyl was close. In addition to being an SF fan, I have a lust for adventure.

In 1986, I'd just begun working on an atlas in which all the maps were the same scale, when there was a science fiction doomsday scenario for real at Chernobyl. The maps helped me understand the scale of what was happening there: had it occurred in England half the country would have been rendered uninhabitable! Russia or the Ukraine had more of the kind of space needed to cope with that kind of event; though those living there could hardly have thought so.

Despite all that it was now, in 2013, feasible to travel there, even if still dangerous; people in organised groups had been going for some time.

My friend Jocelyn and I arrived in Kiev city centre and got in the back of the tour car, while the only other participant sat with the young driver. He was a young Canadian who had turned up at the last moment from Moscow.

We drove north through outlying muddy villages and into open country with more forest the further one went. The skies were cloudy with an occasional lighter patch allowing weak sunlight. It looked more like November than spring. The car had to avoid the odd flood from melting snow and occasional potholes in the road. Moscow was worse, apparently.

Adventurous as I am, I took what precautions I could. I followed the advice about wearing substantial clothing by donning not just my boots, parka and woolly hat but even mittens. Airborne radiation wasn't a problem unless one was sticking around for much longer than a day in some parts.

No, the danger came from ground particles. Thus, it was not a good idea to walk through vegetation or put anything on the ground and pick it up again. Jocelyn was fatalistic, saying that when her number was up it was up. She was the median between my caution and the Canadian who was turning out to be the group nutter. He jabbered away to the driver on the journey up there, ignoring the driver's warning about flourishing his camera at a checkpoint.

Luckily, none of the army or police here took offence and we met the guide: a bald guy with earrings and camouflaged trousers.

A white brick structure with a bas relief of the power station and blue Cyrillic lettering topped by an atom announced Chernobyl itself. The thing to remember about the geography of the region is that the town of Chernobyl is south of the southern end of a man-made lake whereas the power station of Chernobyl is about ten miles away at the northern end, with Pripyat a few miles further. I had my doubts about the habitability of Chernobyl town because the map showed radiation seriously increasing here, marked by checkpoints in and around the town where roads crossed into the zones mentioned.

There were some people still around though, implying that, despite the town having been evacuated at the time of the disaster, it might just about be habitable now.

Chernobyl looked a little strange with pipes here and there constructed gantry fashion up and over the road. That was because ground radiation was already serious enough to make laying them underground or drinking water from them a dodgy proposition. The place was predictably quiet and unkempt too, with plenty of bare trees showing little evidence of spring surrounding detached buildings, residential and otherwise, spacious but none of the more substantial sort usually forming town centres.

A building with a symbolic mural on two adjoining walls: an exploding view of red reactor cores, fuel rods and – surprisingly – birds. A favourite spot to have one's photo taken.

A graveyard of crosses bearing names of villages abandoned in the nuclear disaster.

A vehicle park of irradiated armoured personnel carriers and remote-control vehicles. Safe enough to view from a distance. The remote-control vehicles sported red and yellow colouring that reminded me of Tonka Toys. Even these were affected by radiation where it was high enough; their electronics were fried by it.

A dog wandering around aimlessly without any apparent control. He was a clue as to the state of the wildlife in this region. Animals seemed to flourish here; radioactive dogs or otherwise.

In Chernobyl town we were scanned in a large bare room with a contraption that looked like several metallic phone booths lined end to end without doors. You stepped up into one of them, put your hands on pads and readings were taken.

Not far from Chernobyl power station was a kindergarten. The building's colours were close to monotone and there was a statue at its roadside entrance of a young man with helmet in hand. Originally intended as a memorial to those who died in World War II, it could also have been one to the disaster that had destroyed this place half a century later.

The guide took a reading of ground radiation with a handheld dosimeter about the size of a smallish torch. Airborne it was something like 0.14 microieverts. On the ground it was 24. A lot of snow still lay around under the trees – most of which were still growing in most places – and the guide demonstrated by further readings what an effective shield snow was against ground radiation. Let's test this, I thought, and persuaded the guide to take further readings of areas of snow with brown spots of dirt on them. No increase at all. Then I picked the filthiest pile of slush I could see that you could still barely be called ice. I thought there must be real radioactivity there but the dosimeter only showed a small increase. Effective shield indeed. It was to determine where I would be walking for the rest of this sojourn.

A radioactivity sign stood in front of the kindergarten. To venture inside was to do so at one's own risk. The crazed Canadian did it anyway.

Not much further was the infamous power station itself. Pylons proliferated like a weird, stark forest over the trees. Water stretched in a wide moat down the right-hand side of the road, between us and two cooling towers, the iconic parts of power stations. But one was only partially built.

Number four reactor took up half of the whole lengthy building. Number three formed the other half; a mirror design of number four. At 1.23 am on 16 April 1986, an experiment led to a catastrophic power increase, explosions and fires of a 'roman candle' fashion, according to one account. The result was the release into the atmosphere of radioactive fuel and core materials such as caesium-137, iodine-131 and strontium-90.

At a crossroads between the power station and Pripyat was an anvil-shaped monument flattened into a half arrow. Flowers lay underneath it, as they might do over a grave. In the distance was a pole-shaped construction down a road through heath and the Red Forest, so-called because it had taken so much radiation when the disaster happened that the trees turned red. It looked like a warning for the guide told me one could pick up as much radiation there in an hour as one could normally pick up in a year anywhere else in the world. Just after I was told this, a car happily sped down that road!

Pripyat is about a mile across. It was a modern town built in 1970 for the power station workers. Within a few hours of the explosion, dozens of people fell ill. Later, they reported severe headaches and metallic tastes in their mouths, along with uncontrollable fits of coughing and vomiting.

A ground radiation reading here showed 68.54 microseiverts. It seemed unwise to stay here for longer than a day. There was plenty of snow lying around which I made use of while exploring Pripyat, hoping there were no hidden holes where I was walking and watching my step. This wasn't a good place to fall over.

It was supposed to be unsafe to venture into buildings here because they'd been abandoned long enough to become structurally unstable. There were also spattering waterfalls in and off the buildings here and there caused by melting snow, perhaps picking up dangerous particles on the way down.

That didn't stop the Canadian inspecting what remained of a supermarket. Easy to enter because the glass front had gone. Later he did the same with part of a theatre exposed to the outside. Inside were big paintings of Soviet leaders including a stylized one of Lenin, strangely well-preserved. Could have been stage-managed for tourists, we concluded.

Eventually it was goodbye to the driver too and back to the hotel where I carried out my own decontamination procedure. Off and into bags with everything including the parka, a thorough shower for myself, put boots in shower clear of mat with soles facing other way from me, detach shower head and holding it close put it on maximum pressure to spray blast the boot soles while avoiding spray, do likewise with anything that comes off the soles washing anything that does down the hole, then lastly take bags and boots down to hotel washing and get the lot done!

## 40 Days of This? Talking to Religious Anti-Abortionists at St Mary's Hospital

### Lucy Schorn (2017)

Last week, I met a man called Mike, campaigning to 'end abortion' outside my local hospital, St Mary's. Mike believes abortion is evil. He is part of a worldwide religious campaign called 40 Days for Life, which calls upon people of faith to 'draw attention to the evil of abortion' over a 40-day period through prayer, fasting, vigil and 'community outreach'. He and the two women with him aren't protesting, but praying, so they tell me.

Who can argue with someone simply wanting to pray?

40 Days for Life campaigners don't just pray. Their 'vigil' takes place only a few yards from an abortion clinic, next to a sign that says, 'END ABORTION'. At the same time, they are handing out leaflets that ask you not to 'HURT YOUR CHILD' because, if you do, 'you will later regret it'. Another leaflet is entitled 'Believe in Yourself & Follow Your Heart', followed by the plea to 'Choose Life for Your Baby!' directly underneath.

It seems somewhat dishonest to suggest this campaign is a simple act of prayer. 40 Days for Life specifically targets abortion clinics, staff and patients, and the local community and while it may involve prayer, it is clearly more than that.

I wanted to know more about the views held by Mike and his fellow campaigners on abortion.

What should women whose pregnancies are emotionally or physically dangerous for them or their unborn baby do as an alternative to abortion?

'Reconsider,' said Mike. 'Adoption. There are probably very difficult, trying circumstances for some people, but some people... it's just a way of, "Well I don't want it, so take it away."'

Does Mike advocate the use of contraception to avoid unplanned pregnancy?

'As Catholics', he said – referring to himself and the two women he is with – 'we don't agree with contraception. There's family-planning where you're still open to life, but it's all done with rhythm and cycles and things like that; it's a natural family planning method. And people also say trust in God. If He gives you a child He will give you the means to look after it.'

'Natural family planning' is notoriously unreliable, does not protect against STIs and leaves women vulnerable to illness and complications caused by travel and lifestyle. If this method fails is it then right to refuse women an abortion?

Are there any circumstances Mike and his peers might consider an abortion appropriate, if not essential?

'Very difficult,' Mike said. 'It's not for us to judge but we say it's not right. It's awful but I don't really know. You need the wisdom of Solomon to do that one, but it is very difficult.'

I asked if abortion is appropriate in cases of rape and Mike replied no. 'But that's one in millions,' he said. 'There are loads of babies being killed needlessly. Now, even the law of abortion is flouted. They say it would affect the mental well-being of the mother if she had this pregnancy. Really? You have to have two independent doctors and all this and I'm sure that doesn't always happen.'

Rape Crisis reports that rape isn't quite as rare as Mike seems to think it is. Approximately 85,000 women and 12,000 men are raped in England and Wales alone every year; that's roughly 11 rapes (of adults alone) every hour.

But even putting cases of pregnancy as a result of rape aside, is abortion appropriate if a pregnancy is going to endanger a woman's physical health?

'Yeah, that's another difficult one,' said Mike. 'I'm not sure what the church's ruling or teaching is on that, but basically abortion isn't right.' He continued, 'There are some people who use abortion as a way of birth control: "Oh no, I don't want a baby now and I'm pregnant". So, all we're doing really is just trying to pray.'

There has been a lot of local opposition to the 40 Days for Life campaign from within the local community. Even in the short time I stood talking to Mike, a number of people showed their disgust as they walked past. Pro-choice supporters have counter-demonstrated, holding banners that show support for women accessing the BPAS clinic. I understand more of these actions are planned.

The CEO of Aurora New Dawn, a regional charity offering safety, support, advocacy and empowerment to survivors of domestic abuse, stalking and sexual violence, recently wrote an open letter asking the campaigners to:

'Take a step back from protests outside abortion providers like the clinic at St Mary's Community Hospital in Portsmouth run by the British Pregnancy Advisory Service (BPAS). Like BPAS, I'm asking you to back off: to pray in your own space, or indeed, any space other than outside an abortion provider ... I'm asking you to understand that just as it isn't my right to tell you your beliefs are wrong, it is not your right to attempt to emotionally manipulate, intimidate or scare women on a day that is already difficult enough.'

I wonder why Mike and his fellow protestors feel so strongly about the rights of an unborn child, yet so little about the rights of living, adult women.

As I walked away, one of the women put a small card in my hand and asked me to 'spiritually adopt a child'. At first, I didn't know what she meant, but after looking at the card, I saw that I was being asked to adopt the soul of an aborted foetus.

I found this very upsetting. To pray for women who are not asking for your approval or prayer seems disrespectful enough, as does using the right to protest as a cover for intimidating vulnerable women. But to suggest to a complete stranger and passers-by that they 'spiritually adopt' the souls of aborted foetuses in plain sight of those women is abhorrent.

As I headed home, I had one question in mind. How much of the 40 Days of Life campaign is about the desire to save human lives and how much is simply about wanting to control them?

After talking to Mike, I think I know the answer.

## Not Everyone Chooses to be Childless

### Annie Kirby (2017)

World Childless Week (WCW) aims to reduce the stigma and isolation of childlessness to help people who are childless-not-by-choice – and their friends and families – to find support.

'It took me years to find the support that helped me,' says WCW organiser, Stephanie Phillips. 'If I could let just a handful of people know that they are not alone and perhaps help them find their way to a form of support that little bit quicker, then surely it must be worth a try?'

If you're a parent, if you expect to become one, or if you've never wanted children, you probably think raising awareness of childlessness isn't relevant to you. But WCW also exists to help friends and family better support loved ones who are childless-not-by-choice through what can be an extremely painful and traumatic experience. You might think you don't know anyone who's childless-not-by-choice, but the chances are that you do.

In England and Wales, around 17% of women born in 1970 were childless at the age of 46 (which is the age when the Office of National Statistics considers women to have reached the end of their childbearing years). Statistics vary for women born in different decades, ranging from 10% of women born in 1940 still being childless at the age of 46, to 19% for those born in 1960 and 21% for women born in 1920; averaging out over the last 97 years (for which statistics are available) to approximately 15% of women still being childless aged 46 years. Research from the Netherlands indicates of the women who remain childless, approximately only 10% are happily childfree (i.e. who unambiguously didn't want children). Another 10% are medically infertile, and the remaining 80% are 'childless by circumstance'.

Childless by circumstance includes anybody who would have liked a child but for some reason it just didn't happen. In contrast to the popular stereotype of women concentrating on their careers and leaving it too late to conceive, this category covers a huge range of situations including: having a partner who didn't want children, being in a violent or abusive relationship and deciding not to bring children into that, not being able to afford a child, being widowed, being in a same-sex relationship and so on. (Writer and campaigner Jody Day, founder of support group for childless-not-by-choice women, Gateway Women, provides a comprehensive list in her article *50 Ways Not to Be a Mother*).

Including the medically infertile (some of whom, of course, may have chosen not to have children even if they had been fertile) and those childless by circumstance, that's somewhere between 80% and 90% of childless women who did not happily choose a childless life. From a local perspective, recent population estimates for Portsmouth indicate there are just under 39,000 women aged 46 or above living in the city. If around 15% of these remained childless, that is somewhere in the region of 5,800 women over the age of 46 who haven't had children, of whom about 5,000 did not happily choose to be childless. (These figures obviously exclude women under the age of 46 who already know they will never be mothers due to medical infertility or circumstance, and childless men, for whom no statistics are available – although some research suggests that men are childless at around the same or possibly slightly higher rates than women).

Despite these numbers, we rarely hear about childless-not-by-choice people. Parenthood, or the expectation of it, is the dominant narrative in our society. Consider McCain's 2017 *We Are Family* commercial. 'When it comes to family,' asks the narrator, 'what's normal?' It answers that question by showing families with single mums, stay-at-home-mums, working mums, nans and grans, dads, two daddies, long-distance and weekend daddies, granddads, brothers, half-brothers, friends and sisters. It's a lovely idea, to acknowledge all the different types of families out there, but families without children in them are conspicuously absent. It's symptomatic of a deep-seated assumption that 'family' equals 'children.' We say 'starting a family' when what we really mean is 'having children.' We say something is 'family-friendly' when what we really mean is 'child-friendly.' But I have a family, and so do many other childless-not-by-choice people. It just happens to be a family without any children in it.

If childlessness is dealt with at all in popular culture, the state of childlessness is often 'solved' in some way, for example with the appearance of a miracle baby or an adoption. This airbrushing of being childless-not-by-choice contributes to the stigma of being childless and exacerbates the difficulty of talking about it. This means many people do not how to respond when confronted with someone's childlessness.

A few months ago, I set off to my hair salon in Portsmouth for an afternoon of pampering; just what I needed after a few stressful months making some big changes in my life. The hairdresser, who was new to the salon, listened carefully to my instructions on length and style and after a quick wash and condition, I settled down in the chair waiting to be transformed. 'So,' she said, picking up her scissors, 'have you got any kids?' My heart sank.

The 'do you have children?' question is one most childless-not-by-choice women dread. There's no way to answer without bringing the conversation to an uncomfortable, crashing halt. When I was younger, and answered 'no' to this question, people would often respond with comments along the lines of, 'Well, you'd better hurry up,' or the more snarky, 'Oooh, a career woman.' Now I'm middle-aged, people tend to assume I'm happily child-free. Sometimes people tell me I'm really missing out, or they imply I'm selfish for not having had children. Sometimes I answer, 'Sadly not,' to try and shut down these assumptions in a polite way that doesn't invite too many questions, but it often results in an awkward silence and me crying into my wine at parties, after the questioner has made a hasty exit. I didn't fancy spending the next hour trapped in a stony silence with the hairdresser, so I said 'No,' and hoped she wouldn't pry.

'Oh,' she said. 'So, you've lived a free life.'

Well, no actually. People with children tend to think of the childless as living the lives they led before having children. They imagine the childless perpetually living in their twenties, drinking cocktails and enjoying spontaneous weekends away. But the childless are not fixed in amber – their lives have moved on too, just in a different direction to the lives of those with children. They will have jobs, pets, responsibilities caring for elderly parents and voluntary work. Yes, they might have more time to read books than parents do, or find it easier to fit in their gym sessions. They might even have a high-flying career, but most of them would happily give all this up if it meant they could have a child.

Those who have experienced infertility will tell you there's not much freedom in the devastation of your period coming each month, in painful medical conditions such as PCOS and endometriosis, in the frustration of unexplained infertility, or failed IVF and the expense it entails. They would say there's nothing 'free' in having to smile through other people's pregnancy announcements, scan photos, baby showers and gender reveal cakes, or in losing your friendship group because they all have babies now and you're inadvertently (or deliberately) excluded. There's no freedom in not being booking holidays because what if I'm pregnant by then, what if we've decided to start IVF, what if we get our miracle, what if, what if, what if? For most people dealing with infertility or involuntary childlessness, the miracle never comes. So, no, we don't live 'free' lives.

The reality is that childless-not-by-choice people are at best misunderstood and at worst invisible. This is why World Childless Week is so important. If you're childless, please look at their website for information and support (worldchildlessweek.net). If you're not childless, the website is still a valuable resource to help you support friends and family coming to terms with childlessness. 'Perhaps a parent or two may even read one of the articles and see a glimpse of the world through our eyes,' says Stephanie Phillips.

Not asking strangers if they have children is just one small thing you can do to help (ask what they're doing at the weekend instead – if they do have children you'll soon know and if they don't, you won't have made them feel like a social pariah). Your support will be appreciated, because although we may learn to live with childlessness, the pain of it never really goes away.

## MEP Addresses Air Pollution Danger in Portsmouth

### Emma Murphy (2018)

The #LetPompeyBreathe campaign, organised by the Portsmouth Green Party, Portsmouth Friends of the Earth, Milton Neighbourhood Forum and other local activist groups, is dedicated to improving the air quality in Portsmouth for the health of its residents.

According to Mike Wines, the Green Party candidate for Fratton in the 2018 local elections, the area of Fratton Road, Kingston Road and London Road breaches national targets for its very high levels of nitrogen dioxide ($NO_2$).

Portsmouth City Council (PCC) still has not published its air quality public action plan for public consultation, which was expected by Christmas 2017, following the release of their air quality strategy in July.

The #LetPompeyBreathe campaign has now launched a petition that calls on PCC to publish the plan. As an act of protest, they will erect an air pollution 'graveyard' outside the civic offices at 3.30 pm on Wednesday.

Keith Taylor, Green MEP for the Southeast of England, visited Portsmouth to talk about air quality on November 2, 2017. He and Wines met with representatives from PCC in addition to Dr Jason Horsley, Portsmouth and Southampton's Director of Public Health, and Richard Lee, a regulatory service manager and air quality specialist.

Taylor welcomed the formulation of the action plan, but voiced his concerns about the lack of a timeline for tackling the problem.

He said, 'Every day that passes is one too many for those vulnerable to dirty air. We need to urgently ensure the city is brought within legal pollution limits and made a safer place for pedestrians, cyclists and children walking to school.'

After the same meeting, Wines said, 'We need to see urgent solutions to address the traffic problem in the city. Not just to and from the tourist areas such as Gunwharf Quays, but the traffic problem across all areas of the city such as Fratton Road, Kingston Road, and London Road where residents live, work and learn.'

# How Does the Ched Evans Case Affect Rape Victims and Survivors in Portsmouth?

## Shonagh Dillon and Sarah Cheverton (2015)

**Sarah Cheverton:** Why do you feel the Ched Evans case been so problematic?

**Shonagh Dillon:** Two things are playing out in this case. Firstly, the opinion and assumption that a convicted rapist can just return to his high-profile career having not served a full sentence or shown any sign of rehabilitation or remorse. He denies he committed the crime and is contesting his conviction. As a role model and prominent figure, to resume his career in football seems inherently wrong.

The second issue is the social attitudes towards the case, which are less about Ched Evans and more about the way people think about rape.

The Ched Evans case isn't the first time we've seen this. When Aurora New Dawn [the anti-domestic violence charity Shonagh is CEO of] ran a campaign asking local venues not to book Mike Tyson on his UK tour, we were vociferously attacked for even questioning the idea of placing a rapist on a public and essentially glorified platform in our city, even though his publicly-expressed attitudes to women are so problematic.

The Ched Evans affair is on a much grander scale. I see young men who are happy to tweet that, despite his conviction, what Ched Evans did isn't rape. Those tweets are very worrying because they highlight that these people don't know what consent is.

Look at how the Football Association (FA) have dealt with this case. They chose not to step in at first and make any statement and when they did, they backed Ched Evans to return to football.

No high-profile footballer has come out against him and that could be because there are implications for their contracts. But what about ex-footballers? Or commentators? Where are they? Because the only people in sport I see making noise about this case are women: Charlie Webster, Jessica Ennis – these women are sticking their heads above the parapet and being trolled, threatened with rape, having their families threatened.

That trend, to me, is just as worrying as the case itself.

**SC:** Are there any insights into rape culture that this case has provided?

**SD:** The victim had been drinking, there were two men involved, the victim cannot remember what happened – you see these details used to insinuate the victim can't have been raped. The fact that she was walking upright on video footage has been pointed to in the same way – because 'If you can walk upright, you can't be raped'.

I see people on Twitter saying, 'If all these facts add up to rape, then it must be happening all the time!'

I say, yes, you're right, it is happening all the time. This is the reality of rape in the UK. And it's a particular concern for Portsmouth and the rest of Hampshire because our rape conviction rate is one of the lowest in the country.

With Ched Evans, we can see a lot of attitudes that reveal rape culture like 'She cried rape because she regretted having sex.' That's a big part of how rape culture plays itself out in the portrayal of victims, particularly either as lying about or somehow to blame for the rape.

But the victim didn't 'cry rape' in this case. She went to report her stolen bag at the police station, described what she remembered had happened and the criminal justice system, quite rightly, stepped in and investigated. The police stepped in, the CPS, then a judge and then a jury to find Ched Evans guilty of rape.

What rape culture means for victims like the young woman in the Ched Evans case is that not only are you being accused of all sorts of things that aren't true, but you're trying to come to terms with the fact that you were raped and you don't remember it. Somebody else has to tell you what happened to you.

Let's remember that the victim was nineteen when this happened. She has been named – illegally – in the media. She has been threatened, has had to change her identity and has had to move out of her home. Even after her rapist has been convicted, the media and the public continue to 'retry' the case in the public realm. Even after a jury has established his guilt, it's her behaviour that is being scrutinised, not his.

We blame a woman for the actions of a rapist, dismissing victims as 'sluts' or 'dirty'. There's often no discussion of the rapist at all, only condemnation of the behaviour of the victim. I can't think of another crime where that happens, it's almost exclusive to violence against women.

That tells you where our society is in relation to understanding and making judgments about rape.

There are football chants about this case like 'His name's Ched Evans and he can rape who he wants.' This has been heard at matches.

Let's think about that for a second.

Thousands of people are present. There are women there, children, and you have a crowd confident enough to sing something like that. We crack down, quite rightly, on racist chants in football matches, but chant about rape and no one in the game says anything.

Those people – most often women – who put their heads above the parapet like Jean Hatchet on Twitter are instantly trolled and abused: 'You're a slut, you're a lesbian, you're a fucking man-hater, a feminazi'. It's vicious stuff and each part of it tells us something very important about rape culture.

**SC:** Aurora is particularly active on social media and is very explicit about your feminist credentials. What role do you think that interaction has in the city?

**SD:** When we started Aurora New Dawn, we weren't sure if we could label ourselves as feminist. We had conversations about it. I was adamant that we be an openly feminist organisation. We were born out of feminist activism. We wouldn't be here without it.

So, for me it's essential that we start by labelling ourselves as feminist and being an active part of feminist campaigns. Social media is a big part of that. Our supporters can clearly see who we are and what we stand for from the start.

Social media allows us to invite support from the local community and importantly, it also invites men to be part of the solution.

We're the first domestic abuse service across the county to employ male IDVAs (Independent Domestic Violence Advocates, who work directly with victims and survivors of violence). Nationally, we're also unusual in employing male frontline workers and I'm very proud of that, in part because when I started out working in domestic violence, I was against men training as IDVAs because the majority of victims we deal with are women.

I've changed my mind about that. I realised that men need to be part of the solution.

That's what feminism means to me: you evolve, you change your mind.

Unlike when I first started in the sector, I have a son now and I realise every day just how important it is to have positive male role models. The men who work for us are fantastic and the clients love them. We always offer female clients the choice to work with a woman, but no one has chosen not to work with our male IDVAs so far.

The main thing with social media is that it gives us the ability to engage with the community in a very direct and personal way on a daily basis. We're vocal, we're quite loud, we have a personality and people seem to be responding to that. I hope they always will.

**SC:** Do you think that being an implicitly feminist organisation that is actively engaged with the community has an impact on local victims and survivors of sexual and domestic violence?

**SD:** In everything Aurora does, we aim to act as the voice of victims and survivors. I hope that when we post something that victims and survivors feel strongly about, they feel like someone else has got their back, someone else is prepared to say what they're thinking. I think that can have a very big impact on making sure victims and survivors don't feel alone.

Some of our most popular posts on social media are when we're saying something that perhaps a lot of our followers are thinking but don't feel confident to say. That might be an aversion to being too political on their own social media, or it might be a fear of how their friends might react to a feminist standpoint. High profile activists and organisations aren't the only people who get trolled. Actually, most women and men who place feminist content on their social media are likely to get some form of trolling from within their own communities.

**SC:** What impact, if any, do you think a case like Ched Evans has for victims and survivors of sexual violence living in Portsmouth?

**SD:** I think it's been horrendous for victims and survivors, particularly in terms of the case triggering trauma related to their own experiences of rape and sexual assault. We've had calls from survivors who have been deeply affected by that.

There's been a lot of coverage in the past year of high profile celebrities being accused and charged of offences like rape and sexual abuse. The way these cases are covered in the media has huge implications for victims and survivors on a local level.

In terms of Ched Evans, I think it's particularly horrendous because the coverage is everywhere – every TV screen, every newspaper. It's very hard to avoid it. A lot of local victims and survivors are football supporters, they take their kids to football matches in the city and they'll be hearing about the case in the stands as well.

We're lucky here because Portsmouth Football Club is very active in its community work. We've worked a lot with the club and the players on the White Ribbon campaign, which raises awareness of violence against women in Portsmouth. They've been huge and public supporters. I wonder how the club has to wrestle with that in terms of the stance the FA are taking in publicly supporting Ched Evans. It must make it hard for them to take a stand.

I've wondered how I would feel if, as in Oldham, it was my club who offered to sign him. I'd have a big problem with that because that would bring the issue to the home of the victims and survivors we work with in the city. But the reality is that Oldham ignored the advice of the local Police and Crime Commissioner not to sign him, ignored their MP, ignored Ed Miliband [then leader of the Labour Party]. It wasn't until the sponsors stood up and said they would withdraw funding that Oldham backed down.

I'd be surprised if Portsmouth FC would even entertain a signing like that because of their close links with the community. But when a club does something like that, the likelihood of triggering trauma for local victims and survivors is very high.

Every time I see a new story on the Ched Evans case, I know a victim or survivor is sat at home somewhere in the city watching the same thing and dealing with a flashback of her rape or sexual assault. She may not be sleeping properly or having panic attacks, she may reach for a bottle of wine or even self-harm. Some victims and survivors will be dealing with that trauma in complete isolation because some of them will never have told anybody what happened to them. That makes me feel twice as passionate to let victims and survivors know there are people out there who believe them and are prepared to stand up and be their voice. I hope they know we're here for them when they're ready to come forward.

## From Peru to Pompey: Climate Change is Closer Than You Think

### Lily Anderson-Neyra (2017)

In 1980, at 20 years old, I moved from my birth country of Peru to Portsmouth to be with my British (now ex-) husband. I brought my wonderful baby son and my most precious books. Subsequently in England I gave birth to my lovely daughter.

As a student at the former Portsmouth Polytechnic, I became aware of something called 'Climate Change' around 1985. The subject was discussed among some of the students as a process that came from the Industrial Revolution. I remember a dream I had where the planet talked to me about how much it was suffering as a result of the sadistic, sick treatment it received from humans.

In 2006, I co-founded Portsmouth Climate Action Network (PCAN). We started by organising activities to raise awareness about climate change. Vested interests had started playing with the truth in the late 70s, discrediting the notion that climate change was taking place. So many dismissed the possibility that humans could have a hand in our own destruction. Few knew much about it and some even joked about not having to go abroad if climate change made England warmer.

Indeed. Now, the Brits and other northern Europeans are staying away from many of their usual destinations because of the 'terror threat'. Some commentators have drawn attention to the links between war, climate change and terrorism.

I returned to live in Peru a couple of years ago, but as I write, we are witnessing the effects of climate change. On Wednesday 15th March 2017, Trujillo, the city where I live, saw the beginning of torrential rain and mud slides lasting for a week. Trujillo – located in the desert strip of the northern coast by the Pacific Ocean – used to be nicknamed 'The City of the Eternal Spring'. Now it is inundated with water.

By April 2017, Peru – a country five times larger than the United Kingdom – declared a state of emergency due to flash flooding, mud slides and rain. Several Amazon rivers were placed on red alert status. Peru is very rich in natural resources but – though it might seem strange alongside the current flooding – parts of the country are struggling with the risk of running out of water. A study by the University of East Anglia in 2011 predicts Peru will be the third-worst affected country by climate change.

The lack of funding for a cogent preventative plan to deal with extreme weather also needs to be taken into account when considering the impact of climate change in Peru. Most funding currently goes to emergency response and Peru urgently needs a disaster prevention policy. There are several initiatives by pressure groups to contribute towards setting up an efficient and real policy to help the country face climate change. However, Peru urgently needs to develop ways to better conserve and utilise our water supply and to this end the state needs to commit investment to scientific research, and ensure stronger accountability for how such funding is spent.

If there was ever money to do this, there isn't now.

Corruption is rife in Peru and money disappears easily. As a result, the public is vigilant of local authorities when aid is being delivered, in the hope of preventing it ending up in the wrong hands. Organisations such as the Red Cross Peru seem to be the most reliable.

Recent reports state the floods have left 106 people dead and 364 wounded, while the number of people forced to abandon their homes has reached 156,400. As you read this from Portsmouth, it may seem that climate change is someone else's problem, something happening on the other side of the world to you. But climate change is everybody's problem, everywhere on the planet.

Before the floods started in Peru, we saw sea temperatures on the northern coast rise in some places up to 9 degrees F. The fish that normally swam in these waters went to deeper, colder waters to survive, leaving the sea birds, sea lions and other wildlife that would normally feed on these fish quite literally dying in front of our eyes. There is little we can do to help.

Prior to the floods, many people in Peru didn't want to talk about climate change. I noticed the same phenomenon in Portsmouth when I lived there, and more broadly across the UK. In both our countries, this silence makes it easy for our governments to do nothing, leaving ordinary people no opportunity to prepare until the very worst happens.

News of climate change seems to send people into denial, burying their heads in the sand and hoping it won't happen to them. Tragically, it doesn't work that way.

In the UK, the government has identified an increased risk from heavy rain and flooding, and regards this as a key climate threat. Portsmouth City Council has been undertaking research on extreme weather events since 2000, concluding on its website that, 'future climate change is likely to result in...extreme weather, such as buildings damaged in floods, storms and high winds leading to costly repairs and buildings temporarily closed, or roads melting from hot weather.'

PCC states it owns commitment to tackling the problem in its *Climate Change Strategy.*

I may be writing from the other side of the world, but our hometowns may have more in common than you think.

Why do you think your leaders – in the city and the wider region – are so worried about flood defences they're prepared to pay £105 million for them in a period of Conservative ideological austerity?

If you've ever experienced flooding yourself, lost your home or someone you love in circumstances that were beyond your control, now is the time to start thinking about climate change, before like Peru, the water rises too far.

## St James' Hospital

### John Haynes (2016)

Again I leave the ward and look out through
the windscreen at the bluebells on the grass,
again see Sister's eyes. She'd thought I knew
that if you went home it would be to pass
your last few weeks with him. It would be sad
to separate them, she said in that glass
cubicle with its desk and stubby pad
of death certificates. It would be cruel
too, hopeless as he seems to have been, Dad,
at coping as she put it. But you, you'll ...
won't you? I'll what? I nodded though. Yes, I ...
Bluebells like bluebells in the woods at school.
And then from Fratton Park a massive sigh
filling the clouds and draining down the sky.

## The Inbetween: Following the Track to Fratton Station

### Phoebe Hedges (2018)

It was the end of my first year at university and I travelled home for the summer. Yet each weekend, I found myself spending my student loan to make the three-hour commute back to Pompey. First, it was under the guise of playing Dungeons and Dragons with my university friends. But slowly, I realised this wasn't entirely true. I wasn't making this journey for the city, or a game. Moreover, I realised home wasn't always the place I left behind in Gravesend, instead it was becoming the person I was travelling back to in Portsmouth.

I checked my phone as I stepped onto platform nine at Waterloo East station and willed the free Wi-Fi to work faster and show me the live departures board. There was no time to stop — not in London — so I kept walking up the platform, towards Waterloo. As I reached the top of the ramp, my phone came alive, buzzing with notifications and text messages as the departure board simultaneously loaded. There were three trains to Portsmouth Harbour. The first one left in two minutes. Then twenty-five minutes. The third wouldn't depart for another hour.

Two minutes.

I broke into a run, and forgot patience as I moved recklessly down the right-hand side of the escalator without holding onto the railings. I cut through the crowds of suits and suitcases, and spared a cursory glance at the overhead departure boards to check they aligned with my phone. They did. I kept moving, weaving my way across the shiny tiled floor, and watching as multiple clocks told me I wasn't moving fast enough. I could no longer taste my morning coffee as I charged through the barriers. My heart hammered in my chest and the taste of blood on my tongue replaced the fuzzy sweetness of coffee and vanilla syrup.

Breathless, I threw myself through the doors of the train, and struggled to find my feet as the shifting weight of my backpack threatened to throw me into the other doors. I checked my phone again. On the departure board, there is my train — due to depart one minute ago, DELAYED. I sighed, and slowly slinked off to find a seat, taking it slow after my half mile sprint down the platform.

I settled into an empty four-seater, threw my oversized backpack into the seat next to me, and rebelliously put my tired Converse on the chair opposite. I rested my forehead against the window, staring past my sullen reflection.

My phone vibrated in my hand, reminding me about a text message I had chosen to ignore: 'Good morning. Text me and let me know where you are. I want to meet you at the station.'

I studied the message for a few minutes. The text wasn't unexpected; after all, I was just about to stay with them for the weekend. It read like all their other text messages: straightforward, to the point and friendly.

But just friendly?

Recently, reading Andi's texts had come to resemble a full-time job at Bletchley Park. Each time I reread the message, the creeping memory that I had tried to put out of mind crawled across the skin of my cheeks. The feeling of Andi's prosecco-infused lips on my face last Friday felt more than friendly.

'I've just left Waterloo—google mas says I'll arrive at 12:37– but it's raining, you don't have to come and meet me—we don't both need to get wet ▢ ▢

With Dua Lipa's 'New Rules' playing on my iPod, I tried to make my reply friendly — we were friends — but not too friendly. No one had ever offered to meet me at the station before, but I warned myself against reading too much into an act of kindness. Andi was a good person. They probably offered to meet all their friends at the station. It's just what people do. 'I'll be okay, I've got an umbrella. ▢ ▢t means I can see you sooner.'

I studied this message for longer than three minutes, staring at my screen until it faded to black. I watched my reflection until my lungs began to burn. I was holding my breath. The message wasn't making any more sense the more I stared, or giving me any more answers. I tried to tell myself it wasn't about me at all. Andi was probably just excited to play *D&D* again.

But they wanted to see me sooner. That was more than just friendly, wasn't it?

I chewed my lip as I turned to the window. We left the London suburbs and drove into the England you only see in postcards. I still had a long time to go until Fratton, and instead of wasting time deciphering the enigma text, I focused on the scenery. Rolling hills ran over the horizon, occasionally framed by trees that it was hard to imagine could be anything but evergreen, here in the heat of midsummer.

Rain came and went from the window as the train passed through farmland and lush green fields. Still miles and miles and forty-five minutes till Pompey. I passed stagnant bodies of water and for a week I would adamantly maintain that the long-necked, opalescent, silver bird drinking from one of the murky pools was a crane. I would later be confronted with the possibility that it was a heron, but until then, would remain blissfully awestruck in my ignorance.

I was amazed at the scenery passing by the window. How many of other passengers noticed the menagerie of wildlife I thought only existed on *Springwatch*?

Further along, a fox, healthier than any I'd ever seen in the city, watched the carriages hurtle past. Its coat, shiny and thick, was a glowing amber, broken only by patches of snowy white. Two beady, black, intelligent eyes locked onto mine as we passed, it's head twisting to follow as the train flew past. Then I was gone. 'Just got onto the island—you really don't have to come and meet me.'

I didn't understand why I kept texting Andi, why I was giving them the option to go back on their word. Something in me (experience?) whispered not to get my hopes up. Andi probably wouldn't meet me at the station, they were probably just being polite. 'Too late. I'm already there. ☐ ☐See you soon. ☐ ☐

I flew beneath the Havant Bypass. The girl in the window had a subtle smile at the corner of her lips. I looked past her to snatch a last glimpse of nature before the concrete labyrinth of Hilsea and Fratton swallowed up the train. My smile was nothing in comparison to the hidden stretch of splendour behind the Voyager Industrial Park.

At high tide, shimmering blue water laps the gravel shore. Families of mallards and coots bob along its surface, bills opening and closing as they chatter through the window pane. An occasional dog and its owner out on a walk made me momentarily jealous. The locals know how to get to such a place on foot when I only ever skimmed the surface from the train.

Maybe this was a place to tell Andi about. Maybe we could walk between the wildflowers and the weeds, even if neither of us had a playful golden retriever to give us the excuse.

All too soon, the train slips back into its natural habitat. In the burgeoning white gold sunlight, something is different. Though warehouses still bleed into council estates, and though ratty flags of the St George cross still flap as we fly past, the dilapidated gardens don't look so dead. The smashed-in windows of garden sheds sparkle in the sunlight, the bleakest corners of the city brighten.

Then, finally, the train pulls into Fratton Station, disturbing a roving gang of slate grey pigeons as they pick at the abandoned bones of Ken's Fried Chicken. I haul my backpack over my shoulders, and half step, half fall, onto the platform.

As I begin to climb the stairs, our eyes meet and Andi smiles. Maybe Fratton isn't so ugly after all.

## John Pounds: The Life and Times of a Pompey Legend

### Tim Backhouse (2016)

By the time John Pounds died in 1839, he was, despite his modest lifestyle, arguably the most famous person in Portsmouth. His fame had also spread well beyond the bounds of the old town to the extent that news of his death was reported in London newspapers. He is typically described as the 'Originator of the Ragged Schools', which would have greatly surprised Pounds himself who never accepted that he founded anything. All he did was seek out the poorest and neediest children on the streets of Portsmouth and offer them some food, maybe an item of clothing and, most importantly, an education. The Ragged Schools came later, the first of many in Portsmouth opening at Richmond Place, Portsea in 1849, but the earliest had been set up in Aberdeen in 1841. All such schools claimed to be inspired by the work of John Pounds.

Pounds' life story has been told many times, but none of these narratives captures his voice as well as Henry Hawkes in his *Recollections of John Pounds*. Hawkes, the incumbent at the Presbyterian Church on High Street, was in a good position to write on the subject as he had known Pounds for the last six years of the latter's life.

Although Hawkes writes in a flowery, sentimental style he was nevertheless the only biographer to reproduce on paper the idiosyncratic Portsmouth accent used by Pounds and the children he taught. Thus, when reporting Pounds scolding a child, Hawkes wrote: 'What's y'at, ye rascal there in the corner? I'se pay int'ye if you's not mind, you wagabond.'

Hawkes' reportage gives us an unvarnished, authentic view of the man. From the first time that Hawkes saw Pounds we are left with no doubt about his opinion of the man: '[He was...] rough and self-neglected. He had no hat or coat on. His shirt, very dingy, was open at the collar and chest; the sleeves were rolled back above the elbows. His face, neck, chest, arms and hands; all were dark, as if seldom washed. There was a repulsive coarseness about his features.'

The following Sunday however, the minister saw Pounds in a rather different light: 'He would have been a tall man, six feet high or more, if he could have stood erect, but, as he walked, his body, from the hips to the shoulders, leaned so much forward that his long back was nearly parallel with the ground ... He strode along with determined alacrity ... his legs were long, rather spare, but well-formed and very energetic.'

According to Hawkes, Pounds had transformed himself. He was clean and becoming, the grey hair, billowing out from beneath a broad-brimmed hat, had plainly been combed and brushed. His shirt collar was white, a black stock fitting neatly under it. He wore a well-brushed frock coat and tight, buff-coloured breaches, clean white stockings and polished black shoes. Hawkes came to realise that Pounds always appeared thus when attending church or bringing his scholars to Sunday school. Hawkes returned to the tiny workshop on many occasions where Pounds would get the children to read from the Bible or show the minister examples of long division.

Hawkes later asked Pounds why he had begun to take in children and Pounds explained how he had known a very poor family who had a one-year-old child, born crippled, with both of his feet turned in. Thinking that they would have great trouble looking after such a child, he offered to take little Johnny into his household. Pounds took to calling the boy his 'Neffy' (nephew) and he set about straightening his feet with specially designed shoes which forced the feet into a correct alignment. It hurt the child but it worked.

As Johnny grew older, Pounds realised his Neffy needed someone to play with so he approached his old friend Lemmon and asked him to send some children from his family round to keep Johnny company. In return, Pounds promised to help all the children learn their lessons whilst he carried on his trade mending shoes. After a while, neighbours passing the shop couldn't help noticing the bunch of children happily learning to read and write and they asked John if he would take their children as well. Before long he had up to forty children in his workshop which measured just eight feet wide and fifteen feet long.

In order to educate so many children at once, Pound let the older children, who had already learned to read and write, take charge of the younger ones, whilst Pounds looked after newcomers. It was this method that so attracted the founders of the Ragged Schools and lay behind the idea that Pounds had begun the movement.

Often, during the later years of his life, Pounds would be offered help, both financial and in kind, by the 'respectable' half of

Portsmouth society who understood the importance of his work. He refused to take any money either for himself or for the furtherance of the children' education. He did, however, accept books, though he preferred to have old copies because he felt that, if the pages had come loose, he could pass them out for many children to read at once. His determination to teach only the poorest of the poor was absolute. When informed that two of the children in his care were the sons of a local sergeant major he promptly evicted them saying that their father could afford to pay for their education himself.

Pounds' death at the house of Edward Carter on New Year's Day 1839 is well recorded elsewhere but some of the subsequent events tend to be omitted from those reports. At the time John Pounds collapsed, Dr Martell had been passing by and Carter called him in just in time to see several hands lift the old man into a chair a few moments before he passed away. There was some discussion about what to do with the body and it was resolved that the doctor and one of his pupils would carry it to a fly and take it back to Pounds' workshop. Because of the man's deformities the only way they could transport the body was sitting it in an upright position between the doctor and his pupil and thus they arrived at the old man's home.

The funeral took place the following Saturday, a bitingly cold January day. It seemed like the entire community around St. Mary's Street escorted the coffin to the High Street Chapel where John Pounds was laid to rest in a spot as close to his usual seat in the church as possible. And with the death of the man, the legend began.

# Portsmouth the Corsetry Capital: Feminist Force or Whiff of Desperation?

## Tessa Ditner (2015)

Corsets. A frivolous topic, isn't it? It's like writing about the politics of Dairy Milks. Yet corsetry from the point of view of the city of Portsmouth isn't the same topic as say, looking at film corsetry, 18th Century Marie-Antoinette corsetry, or corsetry in the haute couture studios in Paris. The reason being that the word 'corset' – like all words – doesn't mean anything. Or rather it means lots of different things, depending on where you're standing in time and space.

To Andy Warhol, wearing a surgical corset was a medical obligation after being shot. For Mistress Absolute it's part of her persona, a reminder to her submissives that she's untouchable. For Dita von Teese, a corset is about reflective lighting and curves that you can see on stage or in a large martini glass.

I started this research after reading another Portsmouth writer, William Sutton, and his latest Victorian crime novel, which features a former prostitute in an elegant gown riding a horse, in an age when clothes redefined one's social standing. But for Portsmouth, fame as the corsetry capital comes far later than the Victorian era, with records of corsetry factories mushrooming only in the 1900s (see list below). Indeed, when I asked Portsmouth's history library and Ian Voller of Portsmouth corsetry company, Vollers (established 1899) about the history of corsetry, both describe it not as a garment that disguises or defines social status, but simply as an everyday undergarment.

'99% of women wore corsets in those days,' Ian Voller says. When I ask him what the difference between a sex worker's corset and a high society lady might have been, he hazards: 'Maybe the material would be different?'

As Winifred Cornick, a machinist between 1934-1946 quoted in *Fingers to the Bone* puts it: 'Most of them were just a peach colour, not much white... but the fancy bits you see, they always put ribbon bows on them and little rosy bits. It was the decoration that made it look something.'

That's when I realise that for Portsmouth's corsetry industry, corsets kept your boobs from drooping and your tights from falling. The bit in between the breasts and the hold-ups wasn't important. Having lacing in the back wasn't so your maid could tug until you fainted from fabulous-looking waist compression, but because of the late arrival of the button and zip.

So why Portsmouth? Old newspaper clippings from 1949 reveal celebratory articles over the opening of a new corset factory after bombings. One newspaper article praised factory owners for their new building, reporting the owner's speech at the opening press luncheon alongside a photograph of many (all male) smiling faces.

'500 people of whom 90% will be women...will be carrying out their work in airy rooms admitting the maximum sunlight and air... decorated in peach and rose colours with cream ceiling'. This bizarre women-as-pets description makes me wonder why the *Portsmouth Industries* journalist felt the need to point out paint colour and ventilation. What were conditions like before that being able to breathe was so exceptional?

Portsmouth employed 7000 women in the corsetry trade, some of whom worked from home for a 'family wage' as their children were roped into work as well. The Portsmouth Corset Industry describes the working conditions of corset-makers: 'Wages were miserably low and hours long. There would be fines for arriving late...Learners paid a deposit of 10% and received no wages for some months.'

A stitcher and seamer between 1947-1955, Gwyneth Daly, recounts 'the noise from the machines – it made my head bad the first couple of days I was there. But my Mum said, "Don't tell the managers that's what it was, tell him you had a bad cough," So I wasn't allowed to say the noise of the machines made my head bad, in case I got the sack.'

Machinist between 1951-1957 Joyce Brown recalls 'I do remember one person at Leethems ... She worked on the eyelet machine and put an eyelet right through her finger, through the nail, that was really frightening ... They had to carry her down, she passed out ... I don't really know the outcome of that but there was blood all over the place.'

As the *Portsmouth Papers* of July 1976 explains, 'Stay and corset making exhibited the kind of localisation in Portsmouth associated with carpets in Kidderminster... yet curiously enough the association has never been popularly recognised.' The words 'curiously enough' stick out wonderfully in a piece of journalism: perhaps the real reason for this lack of association is because Portsmouth is ashamed that corsetry did not arise from an overzealous Jean Paul Gaultier designer-type thrusting Madonna on stage, or a post-punk Vivienne Westwood, but as the result of financial desperation.

Sailors' and soldiers' wives received nothing while their husbands were on foreign service despite having families to feed in Portsmouth; and of course, their husbands didn't always come home. Widows were helped by a public fund, but as the Portsmouth Papers point out 'the monies coming forward varied accord to the extent to which a ship caught the public imagination'.

I head to Portsmouth's remaining corset factory, Vollers, to get more of an insight. Ian Voller isn't just the descendant of Harry and Nelly Voller, but also of Sir John Thomas Rowlands, chairman of Leethems (Twilfit) Ltd, who was his great grandmother's brother. Ian's factory is a relatively small space compared to the huge spaces of times gone by. It isn't busy with workers, but there are fleeces on the backs of chairs and joke teddy bears in silly clothes hanging from the wires over the sewing machines, like office workers in cubicles. I ask Ian if Harry and Nelly could be considered sweatshop factory owners.

'It would have been hard work to work in those days,' he concedes. 'But I associate sweatshops with unhygienic workplaces, child labour, cramped spaces and that was never the case.' Ian agrees Portsmouth's corsetry industry grew from its naval ties and the women left behind, but adds one more element: the demand for corsetry was huge. What corset factory owners needed was a town with a lot of spare labour to mass produce like machines. 'Remember these women left behind would have had nothing to do,' Ian says, 'there were no cars, people didn't travel.'

Ian doesn't compare his corsets to haute-couture; he says he's not really into fashion. Instead he compares his corsets to baked beans or Coca-Cola and that, for me, is so very Portsmouth. No airs, no graces but pride, craft and a strong love of history, as can be seen in the Vollers office and the two Victorian corsets displayed there quite humbly, a few steps away from the computers and printer.

So, what now? Now that both the demand and supply of corsets have been moulded into something else by time.

I present Ian with a series of images of corsets I've selected, featured in magazines over the last twenty years. To many of the images, he says simply 'that's not a corset': like the series of metal rungs by Alexander McQueen inspired by tribal neck corsetry. About the famously outlandish corset created by Thierry Mugler in collaboration with Harley Davidson, Ian says: 'Oh, Thierry's people contacted us a long time ago. It was to work on a project together.' He can't remember what came of it, though I hyperventilate at the words: 'Thierry Mugler's people'.

I show him some rubber Gaultier creations and he shakes his head: 'We wouldn't touch rubber.' I expect a complaint about family values but it's actually the process: 'rubber has to be glued and we sew.' At photographs of dresses containing corsets, he doesn't balk, his wife, Corina, later explains that they do bridal and corset dresses as standard. He also doesn't flinch at padding in corsetry but admits it will add to the price of the garment.

Vollers' catalogues are hard bound books, unbelievable in our time of internet shopping. I think Vollers is stuck between two eras. They view corsetry through the eyes of their ancestors, while the rest of us see 'corsets' as a broader church, not caring if it's made of metal, whale boning or paperclips.

Is corsetry a force for feminism? Should we worry that a whiff of desperation still clings to Portsmouth's association with it? There are wonderful quotes in history books: corsetiers talking of camaraderie, going on holiday together and leaving the kids with their men and women boasting of higher earnings than their husband in the dockyard.

But finally, I come across a quote from Maureen Cook, machinist between 1958-1971 saying 'We did the medical things as well, like say if perhaps one person had had a breast off they would have, you know, put a false sort of one in, padded it out with one, but then that bit went sort of back down to another department, but we actually stitched them.' I think of Angelina Jolie standing on the red carpet in a leather corseted Versace dress after a double mastectomy. That's when I decide that corsetry isn't such a frivolous topic after all.

## The Tale of Tank

### John Oke Bartlett (2017)

There is nothing better than whiling away the time in an old pub with a pint of fine ale and some friendly chitchat with the locals. The Nelson, now closed and long since turned into flats, was a particularly fine boozer whose clientele would have me roaring with laughter within minutes of crossing the threshold.

The Nelson's architecture was unremarkable. Built according to a classic template, the pub was interchangeable with many a Portsmouth watering hole. Situated at the junction of Victoria Road South and St Vincent Road, the Nelson Hotel (erected 1898) was part of the building boom that Portsmouth enjoyed towards the end of the nineteenth century. However, prior to this date, the site was occupied by the Nelson's Arms and the Nelson Inn respectively. How sad that neither of these previous manifestations survived modernisation. One can only wonder at what architectural gems have been lost.

The main feature of the Nelson that met your gaze as you came in was the fine old, partially carved wooden bar. The bar faced the front windows with the usual beer engines, upturned bottles of spirits and a heavy substantial wooden shelving unit with Victorian mirror glass. The furniture was commonplace, consisting of wooden tables and chairs which had seen better days. Old wallpaper, ancient framed black and white photographs and the odd mirror or two adorned the walls. To the right of the bar was an arched passageway that led to a snug or lounge bar, which was very rarely used in my day.

The public bar at the front of the building was where all the action took place. Invariably you would find a group of Portsmouth worthies who had fetched up like flotsam and jetsam. These oddities of humankind were welcomed and welcoming at the Nelson, and it was never long before I was being regaled by some preposterous tale which had me guffawing along.

One story has stayed with me. I am not directly referring to a tank but to the nickname of one of the customers who frequented the Nelson, who acquired this moniker many years before as a tank driver in World War II.

The tale of Tank is set in the aftermath of that conflict. Tank and his crew had been on extended manoeuvres, lasting for six weeks or so, in the German countryside and they were looking forward to a pint or two. The military were very much in evidence with tanks and equipment from the Allied forces constantly on the move. The thought of a cool pint kept the morale of his crew going through the trials of filth, muck and lack of sanitation. Finding a suitable hostelry, Tank pulled up in the large car park, which happened to be full of tanks of various nationalities.

The building had escaped unscathed the ravages of the war. The decoration was bright and inviting with large windows overlooking the car park with the forest beyond. Tank and his expectant messmates stepped into the bar to order their first drink for more than six weeks, but they were in for a surprising disappointment.

'Nein, nein,' said the formidable German *frau*. 'You are too dirty, I cannot serve you. Please leave!'

Incensed, Tank and the rest stomped out and climbed back into their tank. Sentiments such as 'Who won the war anyway?' were ringing in their ears. Tank had heard of other crews being refused a drink in similar circumstances, and he had also heard of a solution to the problem.

He swivelled the turret round ninety degrees and pointed the barrel directly at the pub. Not knowing what his intentions were, the alarmed customers, including the matronly *frau*, instantly hit the deck. With a degree of resignation Tank ordered the gun to be loaded with a blank. He fired, smug in the knowledge that his action would certainly put the wind up the snooty frau and her clientele.

What Tank had forgotten was that, whilst there was no projectile coming out of the gun barrel, there was wadding accompanied by a ten-foot flame. He could only watch in horror as the windows of the hostelry disintegrated, the gun flame hitting the back wall and the mirror glass melting in front of his eyes. Tank said he distinctly saw large globules of molten glass dripping down the decimated shelves and pooling on the counter.

Tank instantly accelerated down the road. In his hurry to get away, his turret was still sticking out at a 90-degree angle. As he made good his escape up the road, the row of telegraph poles didn't stand a chance. They were demolished one by one.

As far as he knew nobody was hurt in this escapade. Owing to the diversity of nationalities and numerous tank crews in Germany at that time he was never caught and brought to military justice. However, with his crew sworn to secrecy, not long afterwards an order was circulated throughout the Allied forces that under no circumstances were tanks permitted to fire blanks at German buildings.

The closure of the Nelson brought an end to this particular group of eccentrics who were cast out like so many leaves in the wind. No doubt individually they found some other place to congregate to spin their amusing tales.

## Spinning the Spinnaker

### Sam Ward (2015)

The news broke the way it does these days. Cut-up and quoted, trickling out from the source, repurposed and ridiculed, a William S Burroughs newsfeed. Portsmouth's newly beloved Spinnaker Tower, misunderstood concept piece and yin to the beleaguered Lipstick Building's yang, is going to be sponsored by Emirates.

This city, proud of its rich maritime history, is going to have its biggest monument to that heritage sponsored by a luxury airline company. The usual suspects were there: the flashy press conference and the grinning local politicians sniffing around the corporate bigwig like dogs at a banquet. How did such an unlikely and unsuitable partnership arise? My best guess is that it was an opportunistic sabotage. One council undercutting another.

Sir Tim Clark, godfather of the luxury Gulf state airline, was most probably sat comfortably in the back of his luxury car, being whisked from London to pull off another glorious corporate coup and continue his great services to British prosperity. His destination: a large south coast city with an airport and a football team that plays in red and white, just begging to be rebranded 'Emirates Southampton', home of the historical Emirates City Walls.

Unbeknownst to Tim, Pompey had someone on the inside who quickly got word back to the bosses. A big deal was about to go down in Southampton. They couldn't have that. The people of Portsmouth might be able to survive slash-and-burn Tory cuts, but they would never stand for the city losing out to Southampton. Showing poise and clarity, with a great nose for quick money, the Pompey lot got Harry Redknapp on the blower and he explained to them the ins-and-outs of a last-minute swoop: 'Set up a press conference, get 'em on the dog and bone as soon as you can, and completely outbid the other party, pay well over the odds.'

So that's what they had to do. Get that car diverted and offer Sir Tim Clark of the Realm whatever he wanted – *Whatever Southampton's paying, we'll take half... we'll give you the tower – but our company colours are red and white, we're an airline... Sure sure, whatever you want, it's just the tower. People will understand. It's business!*

That's what I presumed happened, or something equally bungled/sinister (delete as appropriate). Whenever I am forced to think about corporate money mingling with public bodies, I imagine *The Sopranos* meets *The Thick of It*. Desperate scrambling politicians eager to do good by the party and Faustian business executives in well-fitted Italian suits, all oak-panelled walls and brandy decanters.

Then, like the serpent in Genesis, they emerge into the sun, and hold a press conference up the Spinnaker Tower. Councillor Donna Jones and her Conservative council chums gushed about how *good a deal this was for the city* (and great spin for the Conservatives, free to cut away for the duration of their term).

Unfortunately for Donna and co, they underestimated just how much people here in Pompey hate red and white and all that it stands for (until St George's Day of course, that's different). 'It's not about football,' she protested, showing just how little she understands the whole farce. Public spending cuts and budget problems can be dressed up, obfuscated, and hidden. But turning the most visible modern icon of the city into a giant mannequin of a Southampton FC player really isn't going to play well. To get a little serious for a moment, it at best shows a comic lack of connection to the people of the city they represent, and at its worst, and most likely, it shows a wilful ignorance for the petit superstitions of those uppity proles and their games. I wouldn't even put it past them to have done it as revenge for all the income Portsmouth FC lost the city by so inconsiderately being run into the ground by charlatan owners. *Red and White Spinnaker, that'll learn 'em for getting relegated.*

Personally, the colour of the tower is the least of my concerns. What worries me is the precedent the sponsorship deal sets. Removing public funding of services and putting them at the mercy of corporate sponsorship is putting the whole city out to freelance and sell itself to any willing bidder just to secure the public services we should all expect from our council.

This isn't privatisation by the back door, it's going through the cat-flap.

What is most upsetting is that no one cared about that. There was such organised fury against those colour proposals. Such a unified opposition to red stripes on a giant pretend sail that the council has had to reconsider the colour. Only the colour though, not the cuts or the dangerous policy of hinging future services on the eagerness of luxury brands to rename any possible city landmark. No, only the colour.

What I've learned from this saga is that Bill Shankly was right: football is much more than a matter of life and death, and if you can't beat them join them. So, I'm going to head on down to the soon to be Coca-Cola Common and paint one leg blue, one leg red, and start a bidding war on my future.

## Fifty Shades of Dismay

### Siobhan Coleman (2016)

Similar to VCRs, cassette tapes and Adam Sandler's acting career, I have found erotic fiction to be irrelevant for quite some time. This of course is thanks to the increasing accessibility of internet pornography. So, I'm sure you can understand my reluctance when it came to reading E.L. James' naughty bestseller. Whilst the plot of a shy girl meeting an attractive business magnate is tediously predictable, I must admit that a good author delving into the twisted psyche of a sado-masochist could be utterly fascinating. Unfortunately, I have drawn the conclusion that E.L. James is not a good author.

In James' defence, I do not fit into the *Fifty Shades of Grey* demographic and so it isn't surprising that I found the book to be about as titillating as an Ikea instruction manual. Perhaps if I were a middle-aged housewife, whose husband showed more enthusiasm for *Match of the Day* than sex, I would consider seeking escapism in a novel such as this. Furthermore, I must point out that I have never considered myself to be the kinky type. Frankly I am more excited by M&S than S&M.

As 'grey' is frequently used to describe the dullest of skies and dullest of clothing, so too is it used to depict one of the dullest male protagonists in literature. Firstly, 27-year-old Christian Grey is a good ten years too young to be taken seriously as a frightening but irresistible sadist. Call me a radical feminist if you like, but I had difficulty swooning over a misogynist who spends the entire course of the novel pestering a girl to be his slave. But you have to hand it to him, he certainly is silver-tongued: 'I am going to fuck you now.' When compared to characters such as Mr Darcy and Edward Rochester, the uncharismatic Christian Grey holds no place amongst the greatest literary heartthrobs.

As well as my disapproval of the glorification of abusive relationships, I cannot hide my inability to enjoy such inaccurate depictions of sex. I personally don't know anyone who has a sex torture chamber in their own home, but perhaps I'm just out of the loop. 111 pages in, the reader is presented with the first sexual encounter between Christian Grey and Anastasia Steele (which meant I had to endure 110 pages of ball-achingly dull plot before getting to the 'juicy' stuff). Christian agrees to take Anastasia's virginity without forcing her to sign a contract of dominance and submission. Unlike any other female in the world's experience, Anastasia's loss of virginity is painless and results in three orgasms (one of which is obtained by her breast being massaged, who knew right?). I am a firm believer in the phrase 'less is more'. Perhaps if EL James had used subtle and suggestive language it would have had a more seductive effect. However, every sex scene is described through explicit yet horrendously simplistic language. During one particularly obscene sex act, the narrator tells us, 'This is wrong, but holy hell is it erotic.' I do appreciate James' constant reassurance about the erotic nature of the book, otherwise I would never have known.

The book comes to a heated climax (no pun intended) when Christian decides to beat Anastasia with a belt; finally introducing her to the dark world of sado-masochism. Anastasia is left in physical and emotional pain and decides to end her relationship with Christian due to incompatibility. May I remind you that this is a 514-page novel that easily could have been summarised in a few words: woman meets man, man likes kinky sex, woman doesn't like kinky sex, woman leaves man. I opened this review by making a comparison between erotica and pornography, but honestly I've witnessed porn films that have more intricate and complex plots than this.

*Fifty Shades of Grey* is one of the most poorly written books I have ever read. EL James succeeded in creating a mind-numbing story centred on two equally tedious characters who lack any romantic chemistry whatsoever. In my opinion, any author who is inspired by the *Twilight* series seriously needs to re-think their career. I struggled to find any positives in the novel, other than James frequently advocating the use of condoms and the fact that the book only cost me £2.99 from Amazon.

I was stunned to discover the book is part of a trilogy. Unless I find out that the sequel is illustrated, I doubt there is anything that could tempt me to pick it up. I don't suppose *Fifty Shades of Grey* will claim any special place in the history of literature, but it will always be remembered fondly as the book that made menopausal women horny.

## This Too Will Pass:
## A Portsmouth Writer Battles Terminal Cancer

### Gareth Rees (2018)

My life on the run has landed me in hospital. It's my fifth day here and I'm in pain. Troubling, because I've always thought I've merely flirted on the edges of bohemian excess. For years I've been getting up at eight a.m. to do yoga and stand on my head. I took long walks by the sea or in the woods. Then the colour and the zest of the world began to escape me. Food was tasting insipid. I'd stopped laughing in the tavern and was going home without finishing my ale.

Now, in bed on the ward, I just want to cry. But I'm not yet able. Perhaps my childhood training regime saw giving in to emotion as incompatible with running an empire. Once, when I was eight years old, all the cigarette smoke on the bus to school made me feel sick. I got off the bus, vomited and caught the next bus. When I told my father about the incident, he said he was proud of me for not making a fuss. Was I fitting into the 'manly' mould of toughness by staying oblivious to my own distress?

Years later, holding a baby to my breast, I felt manly in a way I'd never felt on the school rugby pitch when, hearing the approaching thud of boots on turf, I wanted to run away instead of catch the ball and get trampled.

It's 10.30 am now. Sun is streaming through the window and I can see over the city to the Isle of Wight. I've been waiting for a scan for four days but keep getting put back on the list because my case isn't considered urgent.

I finally go for the scan and a doctor tells me I can leave hospital. I laugh with joy.

Just as I am getting ready to leave, another doctor calls at my bed. He says the upshot is 'serious'. This time I don't laugh and I don't say anything.

Been at home for five days now. Just played 'Away in a Manger' on the harmonica. And then, just as I am tucking into breakfast, the phone rings. I must go back to hospital for the experts' verdict.

At the hospital a man who exudes professional expertise but is not without a spiritual dimension leans back, smiles and says, 'Of course there's hope. Where would we be without it?'

'Stay of execution' is how I read the verdict. The entirety of life is that way, isn't it? There need be no shock. Yet I am shocked.

I am thankful for calls and text messages conveying good wishes. 'You've met some amazing people,' I think.

One of the callers says, 'Your voice sounds low on animation. There are gong baths.'

'Does someone strike a gong as you're laid back in hot water and lathering yourself?' I wonder. 'Sounds all right.'

And there's still yoga.

A nurse phones and inquires after stools, which I understand to be something other than three-legged items of furniture designed for a sedentary life. 'Are you spiritual or religious?' she asks. I don't think about it, I just say yes.

Lately, settling down for a night's sleep has been like walking through the Valley in the Shadow of Death and desperately wondering where is the Comforter? The hours of turmoil pass slowly. But tonight is different. I munch on a lavender chocolate and then I play 'Silent Night' on the piano.

Though I haven't drunk anything alcoholic for two weeks, on this night I sip a tiny glass of red wine. It doesn't taste good but it soothes me. I fall asleep immediately.

On Christmas Day, I receive passion fruit curd which I spread on a pancake. I give hyacinths.

On Boxing Day, I ponder the value of nutrition to one's treatment. Sometimes the 'it's good for you' ethos – or vice versa – only adds anxiety. Is too much anxiety more injurious to health than even bacon, egg and fried bread?

My next hospital appointment is to discuss a policy of meeting aggression with aggression. It's like calling in the air force to bomb a terrorist den. Maybe the enemy will be annihilated or some of them will escape and stir more trouble elsewhere.

I will probably lose my hair, Doc Delilah tells me. I call him that because of wicked Delilah in the Bible who, by arranging for Samson's hair to be shorn while he slept, destroyed the spell that had helped him vanquish enemy armies all by himself. Strength gone, Samson was delivered up to his enemies. But after some earnest praying, the strength came back to him.

I feel on the run from the cold. I go out to buy V8 juice and rush home into my warm bed. My mind is occupied by a Victorian novel, the Premier League soap opera or cricket from Australia. However, distractions can only distract for a while.

The distraction of the nightly routine of visiting the tavern is no more. Release can be confused with freedom. I may be free of one form of incarceration but once I'm out of my cell, there is a big question about how I use my freedom. Thinking becomes unbearable, morbid. I have an attack of morbidity tonight.

I wake to find my consciousness altered. The 'real' world as I've supposed it to be, the world of the familiar seems distant. 'Is this dying?' I ask myself. Then I recall the licks of cannabis oil I took before bedtime. My heaven-sent supporters went to great effort to procure this 'miracle cure'. Initially, I resisted because I didn't want my mind to be tempted down the dark, gnarled path to paranoia. But last night I tried some and perhaps that's why I am in this state now. Instead of crying out for help like the lost child I feel myself to be, I calm myself by saying, 'This too will pass.' And it does.

All my life I've thought I'd get unwell and then get better again. But there must come a time when you don't get better and it will be your body that passes.

As I lie in bed one afternoon, I listen to *Gardeners' Question Time*. A woman in the audience complains that a badger has dug up her maple tree and that, since re-planting, it had failed to prosper. An expert says the maple tree is suffering from post-traumatic stress disorder. Aren't we all to an extent? It's another reason I'm only partially alive. The rest of me is still stunned by the shock of arriving into this world.

At the end of the programme, a man says, 'Don't forget that because we're gardening, we're happy people.' Blessed are the gardeners.

My next appointment in the vast hospital. I'm concerned by the bigness of the medical system, its logic of centralisation. It was the same problem when I was working as a teacher. Schools trebled in size. Teachers couldn't remember the names of the children they taught.

Blood pressure reading. Injection. Waiting room. Take out a book about cherry and apricot trees in a small-town garden in Hungary in the 1930s. A mother sewing Stars of David onto clothes. Dark clouds lowering over childhood. And the author writes of his father that he must have 'studiously cultivated detachment to delude himself into believing that somehow he stood outside events.'

Later I replace my clothes with a loose gown and am conducted to a bed with much machinery around it. Three uniformed people operate on me. I yelp a couple of times and then I can go home. On the way out of the hospital, I buy a mango smoothie. It is the most wonderful thing I've ever tasted.

I see the GP the next day. Her sense of humour seems a long way off. She uses words like 'incurable' and speaks of a morphia future. Her logic is that, if an invasion force has progressed, it will continue to progress. That's not scientific, is it? Maybe the invader will tire and retreat. The doctor recommends a supine capitulation to pain, which can be allayed but will, in the end, choke out life.

Had she employed that euphemistic formula about getting your affairs in order, I would have laughed. My affairs have never been in order. Why should that change now?

Yet all my life I've dreamed of inner conflicts resolving themselves into peace. Now that prospect seems more remote than ever. Perhaps I've wrapped myself up with the dubious comforts of this world so much that I've forgotten another world. I wonder even if there is another world. Is there anything left after the demise of the body? Is the future oblivion? Not an enticing thought. Would it not also contradict imagination?

Although I'm hungry, what I eat tastes poisonous after a few mouthfuls – unless it's sweet. I could eat custard, ice cream and chocolate all day. In hospital I could eat puddings all day if I wanted. Yet voices tell me sugar, especially of the refined white variety, is the greatest enemy. It's craved by the force that's working for my demise. I'm still, it seems, pretty much an addict.

The Dalai Lama said life is a preparation for death. I'm inclined to agree. I want the comforts of this world but they have become distractions and ancient attachments acquired in childhood, like competitive sport. The Six Nations rugby tournament starts tomorrow but I'm not interested anymore. Seems so unevolved, deriving elation at the price of another's desolation. Surely, I should be seeking harmony by this point in my life.

Sometimes I pick up my guitar or the harmonica, or play some chords on the piano. Always feel better when I do.

We are now in February and it's premature to start saying spring is here. I buy some daffodils anyway. The scent breaks the straitjacket of mundanity and lets me into heaven for an instant.

While I'd like to trip out to the Meon Valley and spot some snow drops, I'm too weak for outings. Is this the way it's going to be from now on? The question scares me. I think not of the fields of Elysium but the Big Dark. That too will pass, I hope.

## Things to do Around Southsea

### Maggie Sawkins (2015)

Sit where Steve Tebb, Drainman of Portsmouth, sat,
watch the dancing sea. Reminisce the Wild Mouse,
the Wall of Death, Uncle Charlie's tattoos.
Get married for the third time. Launch a book of poems.
Drink champagne at The Queen's. Go for a curry.

Watch Syd Little in Cinderella at The King's.
The Spinnaker Tower lit up for Christmas.
Love Albert Road! Go for a curry.

Take Amber Leaf and Milky Ways to a friend in St James'.
Think about the man who stole a turkey from Tesco's.
Lend someone a score. Talk to seagulls. Play crazy golf.
Listen to the cursing sea. Go for a curry.

Take a red geranium to Bett at St Vincent's,
watch Des O'Connor on plasma TV.
Fly a kite on the common.
Consider a swim. Go for a curry.

Watch Red Arrows draw love hearts over South Parade Pier.
Buy okra and cardamoms from Akram's for later.
Put change into the Bangladeshi welfare tin.
Collect Robin from the hover. Inhale the sea.
Have a glass or three at The Phoenix.
Talk about times. Love Albert Road! Go for a curry.

See Angelhart Quartet at The King Street Tavern.
Disgrace oneself in an Aqua taxi.
Sleep it off. Write a poem. Go for a curry.

# Biographies

JS Adams is a writer, artist and musician who has ping-ponged in and out of colleges and universities over the last twenty odd years, studying computer programming, physics and the creative arts. He formerly lived in London and toured in a rock band to Manchester, Dublin and Austin, Texas.

Dr Dave Allen was born and raised in Portsmouth, and was briefly a professional 'pop' musician before going on to lecture at the University of Portsmouth and conduct research into local music history and Hampshire County Cricket Club, where he is the Archivist.

Lily Anderson-Neyra is a former Portsmouth resident and co-founder of Portsmouth Climate Action Network.

David Angus is a travel writer, photographer and planetary modeller who has worked for the BBC amongst other organizations.

Tim Backhouse was a tireless chronicler of Portsmouth history who researched and wrote about everything from local cricket in the nineteenth century to the city's role in World War I. His websites include History in Portsmouth and Memorials and Monuments in Portsmouth.

Lewis Baglow is a writer and graduate of the University of Portsmouth's creative writing programme. He is currently a freelance journalist for the Bonus Stage website.

John Oke Bartlett trained at the Rose Bruford College of Speech and Drama and worked extensively in the professional theatre for ten years. Whilst lecturing in drama, he developed an interest in directing and writing. *Star & Crescent* has given him the platform to supply several memoir pieces. He has written many plays including *Hess*, which explores conspiracy theories surrounding the World War II flight to Britain by Rudolph Hess. A prolific folk singer/songwriter, he has published CDs and a songbook entitled *Patterns in the Sand*.

Denise Bennett, MA in Creative Writing, runs poetry workshops in community settings in Portsmouth and her collections *Planting the Snow Queen* and *Parachute Silk* are published by Oversteps Books. Read more of Denise' work at Poetry PF.

James Bicheno writes historical fiction and alternative history and has recently started script writing. He has had short stories published in various anthologies.

Richard Brooks is a freelance author living in Southsea. His latest book *The Knight Who Saved England* is a biography of William Marshal (c.1147-1219), Earl of Pembroke, Regent of England, and a frequent visitor to Portsmouth.

Rosy Bremer is implacably opposed to war as a means of communication and nuclear weapons as a means of world domination, and grapples with these issues and others in her writings for *Star & Crescent*.

Alan Burgess is a Portsmouth resident and activist, and works as the media officer for Unite the Community.

Jack Caramac is a Portsmouth-based visual satirist.

Reg Chrettyn is the pen name of Professor Sir Willoughby 'Willy' Montague 'Ginger' Featheringstone-Howe (Baron Featheringstone-Howe of Glumley), a man so upper-class that he has two nicknames. Featheringstone-Howe was educated at Eton College, where he won the Strafford and Bowman Shakespeare Prize, and at All Soul's College, Oxford, where he completed a DPhil in late Victorian Decadent aesthetics. He was elected the youngest fellow of that college since 1527. He currently holds professorial chairs in English Literature at Oxford, Cambridge, Yale and Harvard Universities. He was made a life peer by the British government in 2011.

Jon Crout is a Portsmouth native and resident with an enthusiasm for words and stories that means he writes short stories, a very occasional blog, and has performed on stage at both Basin's Dancehall in the Tricorn and the Gaiety Bar on South Parade Pier.

Sarah Cheverton is Editor-in-Chief of *Star & Crescent*, Writer in Residence for Hampshire charity Aurora New Dawn and has written for a range of outlets including *Red Pepper, Huffington Post* and *Women's Views on News*.

Siobhan Coleman studied English Literature and Creative Writing at the University of Portsmouth and loves writing satirically on topics such as religion, politics and gender inequality.

Cal Corkery is involved with several local activist organisations such as Portsmouth Against the Cuts Together (PACT) and Momentum Portsmouth.

Jackson Davies is a spoken word poet who occasionally dabbles in Photoshop and design work when spurred into action by an interesting brief. He lives in Southsea with his wife Sarah and his daughter Martha.

Shonagh Dillon is a passionate advocate of women's rights, who has worked in the violence against women sector in a number of roles and who founded Aurora New Dawn in direct response to public sector cuts.

Tessa Ditner is a writer and creative writing lecturer. She was the Contributing Editor of *Skin Two Magazine* for several years and editor of the short story anthologies *Portsmouth Fairy Tales for Grown Ups*, supported by Arts Council England and *Octomorphosis*. For more info visit her website tessaditner.com.

Dianna Djokey is a curator and museum educator who works with connecting the public with museums and their collections, in her spare time Dianna writes about culture, social and communal matters.

Abigail Gilchrist and Jo Willoughby are members of *Stair/Slide/Space*, a Portsmouth based group of artists and curators that work collectively to foster research and concept-led artistic practice.

Mike Gumbrell runs a health care charity based in North End and studied Politics, Philosophy and Economics with the Open University.

Dr Alison Habens is Course Leader for Creative Writing at the University of Portsmouth and the author of *Dreamhouse*, *Lifestory*, *Pencilwood* and *The True Picture*, as well as academic articles, poetry and plays.

Dr Stephen Harper is Senior Lecturer in Media Studies at the University of Portsmouth whose latest book is *Screening Bosnia: Geopolitics, Gender and Nationalism in Film and Television Images of the 1992-95 War* (Bloomsbury, 2018).

John Haynes is a poet, teacher, lecturer and winner of the Costa Award for Poetry 2006 and the Troubadour Poetry Prize 2007. John teaches creative writing for the Workers' Educational Association in Portsmouth.

Phoebe Hedges is a freelance writer and aspiring poet, currently working as a contemporary romance ghost-writer in between her studies at the University of Portsmouth.

Graham Horne served in the British Army in the 1970s and is now a member of Veterans for Peace.

Suzy Horton worked in education for most of her life, teaching in inner-city London schools and serving as the deputy head of a primary school, before becoming a Senior Lecturer at the University of Portsmouth. She is now also a councillor and the Cabinet Member for Education at Portsmouth City Council.

Samuel H James (higgy_) is a 'digi-collage' artist and has been writing, recording and producing music for 12 years. He has performed at events such as Southsea Fest 2016. You can find more of his visual art work on Instagram under the handle @higgy_ and his music is available here, here and here.

Margaret Jennings earned an MA in creative writing at the University of Chichester in 2001 and reads widely at poetry events. Margaret was longlisted for the Bare Fiction Literary short story prize 2014.

Annie Kirby is a writer and writing tutor. She won the Asham Award for her short story *The Wing*, and her work has been anthologised and adapted for broadcast and audio download. Her non-fiction work has appeared in various outlets, including *The Guardian*. She blogs about childlessness-not-by-choice at *The Imagined Mother*.

Andrew Larder is a mature student at Portsmouth University, where he studies Creative Writing and Film Industries.

Helen Larham is a poet living and working in Portsmouth: contributing to poetry magazines, taking part in poetry workshops and performing her work at *Tongues and Grooves* poetry venue.

Christine Lawrence holds an MA in Creative Writing, writes regularly for *Star & Crescent* and is the author of the novel *Caught in the Web* (CompletelyNovel, 2012).

Christine Lord is a highly experienced journalist and broadcaster whose book, *Who Killed My Son?* (CreateSpace, 2013), recounted her son Andrew's death from vCJD, the human form of 'Mad Cows' Disease' and her subsequent investigation into the BSE crisis.

Justin MacCormack is a short fiction author whose work has appeared in several horror and sci-fi/fantasy publications, and his first collected works, *Hush! A Horror Collection* enjoyed a brief stint on the bestseller charts. He is the founder of the *Portsmouth Roleplayer's Guild* and manager of the popular gaming website Dog with Dice in which he writes articles, editorials and reviews. Justin has recently worked on a series of LGBT erotica comedies with Dark Desires Press, called *Tales of Monsterotica* and includes titles such as *The Castle of Count Shagula* and *Bite of the Queerwolf*. Yes, really.

Emma Murphy is a queer British freelance writer specialising in politics, travel, and entertainment. She is the co-editor of the Green Pompey blog and has a first-class BA in Journalism from Edge Hill University with accreditation from the National Council for the Training of Journalists. Her claim to fame is that Barack Obama (yes, that one) follows her on Twitter and she's never been sure why. She takes her coffee seriously and wears odd socks because life's too short.

Stephanie Norgate has had two books of poetry published by Bloodaxe Books: *Hidden River* (2008, shortlisted for both the Forward Prize for Best First Collection and the Jerwood Aldeburgh First Collection Prize), and *The Blue Den* (2012).

Dr Van Norris is Senior Lecturer in Film and Media at the University of Portsmouth whose latest book is *British Television Animation 1997-2010* (AIAA, 2014).

Sir Eugene Nicks MA, QC, KBE is Policy Adviser to the All-Portsea Conservative, Regressive and Imperial Association (established 1799). He was born at some point in the early part of the twentieth century but cannot remember precisely when. His hobbies include practical Social Darwinism and waving £50 notes in the faces of Portsmouth's vagrants.

Claire Pearse is a Creative and Media Writing graduate of the University of Portsmouth who enjoys writing about her interests which include LGBT+ rights. She aspires to educate audiences through her writing.

Richard Peirce is a teacher, trades union activist and poet, and has travelled in Western Europe, Russia, Turkey, Thailand, the Philippines, China (for afternoon tea), Tanzania, Kenya, the USA and the Isle of Wight. His poems have been translated and performed in Romanian and Spanish.

Tom Phillips is a freelance writer and lecturer whose work encompasses poetry and theatre, journalism and travel writing, and has been published in a wide variety of magazines, anthologies, pamphlets and in a full-length poetry collection *Recreation Ground* (Two Rivers Press, 2012).

Emily Priest is a reviewer, reporter, editor and social media guru for *Star & Crescent*. She also writes poetry, travel writing and blogs at *Emily the Writer*.

Gareth Rees (1948-2018) was a Contributing Editor to *Star & Crescent*, whose other work appeared in The Guardian, The Contemporary Review and the 2014 collection *Read Rees*, published by 137 Albion Road.

Maggie Sawkins won the 2013 Ted Hughes Award for New Work in Poetry for her live literature performance *Zones of Avoidance*. She is the founder of Tongues & Grooves, Portsmouth's popular poetry and music club, which has been going since 2003. Her website is www.hookedonwords.wordpress.com.

Lucy Schorn is a writer, feminist and mum, born and brought up in Portsmouth. She started the feminist blog *Savage Fringe* and is passionate about the rights of women and the LGBT+ community.

Shelagh Simmons spent most of her working life in the public and voluntary sector. A strong opponent of the US/UK invasion of Iraq, her comments were included in the Parliamentary Inquiry into Foreign Policy Aspects of the War Against Terrorism. In 2016, she graduated as a mature student from the University of Portsmouth with a degree in English and Creative Writing.

Sudip Sen is a former government lawyer and now a writer and researcher based in Portsmouth.

Sue Stokes is the coordinator of the Southsea Green project and has worked in Hampshire delivering the Children's Fund and Children's centres, which wrap care around families like all good communities should, and that are sadly diminishing in areas who need that extra support.

William Sutton is a novelist, journalist, musician, Latin teacher and University of Portsmouth lecturer living in Southsea, whose latest book *Lawless & the House of Electricity* (Titan, 2017) tackles Europhobia, immigrant panic and mental health issues in a Gothic country house.

Dyanni Swhyer-Brown is a South London-born graduate in Creative and Media Writing at the University of Portsmouth who now blogs at Twenty Going on Twelve.

Dr Tom Sykes is a widely published author, travel writer and literary journalist; Founding Editor of *Star & Crescent*; and Senior Lecturer in Creative Writing at the University of Portsmouth. His latest book is *The Realm of the Punisher: Travels in Duterte's Philippines* (Signal Books, 2018).

Paige Tabone is a graduate of the University of Portsmouth who blogs at *alifelookingup*.

Keith Taylor MEP is a Member of the European Parliament for the South East England region. Keith is the Green Party's spokesperson for animal protection and a member of the EU Parliament's Intergroup on LGBTI Rights. Keith is active across Hampshire including campaigning to improve air quality and halt oil and gas drilling.

Kelly Turner is a student at the University of Portsmouth who spends her free time writing, particularly poetry. She hopes to have a career in journalism, but also has an interest in the film industry.

Claire Udy is an independent socialist councillor for Portsmouth City Council, a mature student at the University of Portsmouth and a regular contributor to *Star & Crescent*.

Maddie Wallace is a Southsea-based blogger who writes about her experiences with breast cancer and the challenges of raising sons as a single mother.

Sam Ward is a writer and graduate in American Studies whose academic focus is on cultural representations of oppressed groups and their resistance.

Richard Williams is a poet and photographer whose work has appeared in magazines such as *Acumen, Orbis, Envoi, Brittle Star, South, Frogmore Papers* and *Poetry Monthly*.

Matt Wingett wrote episodes of Thames TV's police drama *The Bill*, as well as national newspaper articles and stories, before becoming an author, publisher and historian whose latest book is *The Snow Witch* (Life is Amazing, 2017).

Dr Sophia Wood completed her PhD thesis entitled *The Holocaust and Popular Culture* in 2005 and has is now Senior Lecturer in Media Studies at the University of Portsmouth.

Mark Wright is a writer, editor and journalist who reported on the 2017 General Election for *Star & Crescent*.

## Acknowledgements

*The deepest possible thanks* to *all our contributors* featured in *Pompey Writes*. How lucky we are to have so many adept and talented creatives in this great city.

We're also hugely grateful to Emily Priest, *Star & Crescent*'s chief reporter, designer and social media guru, for her peerless marketing and design skills; Dan McCabe for his beautiful cover design; Matt Wingett for doing such a wonderful job of printing and publishing this book; and to Joni Rhodes, Emma Jones, Jo Russell and their colleagues in the Faculty of Creative and Cultural Industries (CCI), University of Portsmouth for smoothly managing the logistics of what has been a large and complex project.

This book was only made possible with a generous grant from CCI. Particular thanks must go to Trevor Keeble, Joan Farrer and the rest of the awarding panel who kindly agreed to invest in the project that we all hope will bring immense benefits both to the faculty and to the wider creative scene in Portsmouth.

And, finally, thank you to all who have read, viewed and interacted with the *Star & Crescent* website since its inception in 2015. It is because of you that the debate has remained so lively, urgent and intelligent.